Of PRAYERS *and* BEATINGS

GERALDINE CYNTHIA FORTÉ

NEWMAN SPRINGS PUBLISHING
320 Broad Street
Red Bank, NJ 07701

First originally published by Newman Springs Publishing 2018

ISBN 978-1-64096-297-2 (Paperback)
ISBN 978-1-64096-298-9 (Digital)

Printed in the United States of America

A Daughter's Prayer

Oh, Daddy, dear Daddy ... I have forgiven You
I believe you always loved me, I really do
Your lifetime of suffering alone must have been great
So much anger, distrust, and resentment on your plate
To live most of your life beset by fears
That your secret could resurface after so many years
Oh, Daddy, dear Daddy ... I do understand
You are relieved of your fears ... Here, hold my hand
Let us pray together on bended knee
Pray that peace is finally yours ... throughout eternity

Prologue

HERE I AM AT SEVENTY-THREE years of age, getting up to go to work every day. After thirty-seven years, I retired from public education at the age of sixty, taught at two different universities since then, and now, I am employed by the California Women's Institute at Chino. I teach a creative writing class to the female inmates who are part of the Violence Abatement Counseling Program. What a joke! These women were violated, some from the time of childhood, and the violence that led them here was in many cases an act of desperation or protection. The majority of these women are incarcerated here because they took the life of someone who was either abusing them or abusing someone they wanted to protect. One of my favorites is Samella.

Samella received a twenty-five-year to life sentence for clubbing her estranged husband in the head with a Dutch oven. He had brutally beaten her for years, and when he finally left her for another woman, she thought that she was free of him. Not so. The other woman put him out, and he had broken into Samella's home. He severely beat and kicked her with enough force to crack three of her ribs, and then he finished off his evening's work by raping her. He slept for about an hour beside Samella, who was in excruciating pain and afraid to move a muscle for fear that he might attack her again. When he woke, he went into her kitchen, rummaged around in her refrigerator for something to eat, and he was about to walk through the front door when Samella slammed the cast-iron pot into the back of his head. She was convicted of voluntary manslaughter due to a plea-bargaining deal—from murder one down to voluntary manslaughter. The prosecution stressed that she was not under attack at the time that she willingly picked up a weapon and used it for mayhem against her husband. Had she struck him while he was in the act of beating or raping her, it could have been considered self-defense.

Within the group counseling program, the women are placed into therapeutic units depending upon their strengths and interests. Some of them are in the culinary arts program, and they create the most interesting and exquisite confection items I have ever seen, such as a fifteen-tier wedding cake decorated with both silk and butter cream roses. Some of them are in the needlepoint program; and they knit, crochet, and stitch their way into some semblance of calm while discovering the foundations of the rage that brought them here. Some of them are in the ceramics program, and they are constantly amazing me with the things that they create and paint. Some of the things look like animals, people, insects, or flowering plants. Some of the things look like they migrated from Mars.

The ladies in my particular program are composers. They compose poems, songs, short stories, sermons, prayers, and a couple of them are working on novellas. They are encouraged to share with each other, and one day, Samella looked at me and said, "Hey, Dr. Cleo! We know that you have been composing your family's story for quite some time. Why have you not shared your composition with us?"

I decided, "Why not?"

CHAPTER 1

Cleophus

SOMETHING WOKE ME UP AROUND 3:45 a.m. that day, and when I looked out of the window, I observed the muted red sheen on the moon. It was beautiful yet foreboding, and I felt that there must be some special meaning for its existence.

"They say that when the moon is red like that, some blood is about to be spilled, and someone is going to get killed."

Brother had also awakened and was standing next to me, staring at the spectacle. I didn't believe in those old folks' tales, and since colored folk could not go into the City Library in 1938, I planned to go to Reverend Washington's home over the weekend to look up the scientific meaning for a red moon in his reference books. From those books, I would get the real story on the "red moon" phenomenon. I didn't fault Brother for his belief. He was my father's firstborn son, and he was destined to think and act just like him. That meant believing the same old folks' tales also. We went back to our warm beds and slept comfortably for a couple more hours. By the time we made it downstairs, Sister was already in the kitchen with Viney, making preparations for the day's meals.

That was early this morning. It is now evening, and instead of being warmly wrapped in my mother's handmade patchwork quilts, I am lying on a mattress of burlap sacks, and I am entombed in a makeshift hiding place under a load of wood planks on their way by truck to the big city of Meridian, Mississippi. I was going to try to

make it on foot, but they insisted that I travel as quickly and as unobserved as possible. In the place of a headboard and foot board, there
were four 24×24-inch cement blocks, two at each end, whose sole
purpose was to support the wooden door over my body, separating
me from the load of wood planks that were loaded onto the truck.
It was dark in my tomb, and it was cold. Something kept biting me
on the toe, but since I could not bend down, I couldn't do anything
about it. From time to time, the truck lurched or rode over a bump
or pothole, and did that hurt! I dare not relieve myself while in my
tomb because I would have to lie in it for untold hours, and it would
have added to the discomfort of the cold. I could only imagine how
painfully uncomfortable the ship travel through the Middle Passage
must have been for the kidnapped Africans on their way to bondage
in the United States. They traveled shackled on top of each other for
months. I only had to endure my torture for a number of hours. My
choice was to accept this method of travel, period. You just did not
argue with my father once his mind was made up. I could not sleep,
so I reticently pondered over the events that had brought me to this
time and this place.

CHAPTER 2

Cleophus

I AM CLEOPHUS GEORGE DUARTÉ, second son of Scripture and Arnetta Duarté. My father, Scripture Duarté, was a proud black man. A Methodist by faith, a farmer by profession, a family man, and a man with skin as black as coal. His wife, my mother, Arnetta, was a brown-toned woman, selected as much for her skin color and long hair as for her submissive ways. She allowed him to reign as the head of his household, made sure that his house was kept clean, his children orderly, and food prepared just the way he liked it. If she failed in any one of her tasks, she could be sure to get a sound beating from Scripture. Therefore, she ruled her household as Scripture ruled her. If he beat on her for not completing a task to his satisfaction, she beat on the kids—starting with the two eldest. These eldest of the nine children had the tasks of keeping the others in line—usually with a sound beating or the threat of one.

The Duarté clan originated in the 1820s when the first two brothers, George and John, were purchased as slaves from the Bahamas by a Portuguese plantation owner named Duartés. They quickly learned the language (a mixture of English and Portuguesa), the slave lifestyle, the tenets of the Methodist religion, and the consequence for being disobedient or embarrassing their owner. Senhor Duartés considered himself to be a good plantation man. Many of the plantation owners in Mississippi had to replace slaves annually to make up for the ones that had been beaten to death, hung, burned, hunted and killed by bullmastiff dogs, drowned, or maimed during a severe disciplinary act. Senhor Duartés rarely had to beat his blacks for they intuitively knew how to behave. They never attempted to run away, steal food, sass him or his wife, embarrass him, or slack off from their workloads. He fed them well. Each working black received grits and black coffee for breakfast, a noontime ration of cornmeal mush, boiled beans, hoe cakes, and more coffee. Dinner would be a healthy serving from whatever cauldron of vegetables had been relegated into a virtual soup after simmering over a low fire all day: greens, cabbage, or green beans along with a potato, turnip or rutabaga and cornbread. On Sunday mornings, they got a helping of fried fruit (peaches, apricots, apples or plums), biscuits, and bacon along with the grits. This had to keep them going until after the morning church service and after the whites had been fed. Then they would be allowed to partake of whatever cuisine had not been served to the whites or devoured by the dogs.

Some of the old-timers remember the time that Senhor Duartés had to beat the hell out of two of his blacks. It was a Sunday. The overseer had arrived with the blacks in time for the church service. They always took off a couple of hours prior to the start of the service since they had to walk while the overseer rode a horse. The Duartés family rode to service in the family wagon, as was the tradition for slave-owning whites in Newton, Mississippi, at that time. In the sanctuary, the blacks were given a portion of the floor in the front of the pews, where they were required to sit quietly during the worship service. If they had to leave the room for a nature break, they had to raise the right index finger, requesting permission from the overseer. They had to relieve themselves in the nearby woods, wash their hands with creek water and laurel leaves, and get back into the sanctuary within the specified amount of time. None of Senhor Duartés's blacks ever tried to run away, so he did not require the overseer to accompany any slave to the woods for this purpose. The service went on until about 1:00 p.m., and then the white folk filed out in order, shaking the minister's hands and greeting his family in the customary fashion. They reassembled in the social hall and, on exceptionally warm days, out under the trees for the afternoon repast. Slaves had spent the better part of Saturday preparing the repast, for the Methodists practiced that there was to be no work done on Sundays—other than the blacks serving the whites and cleaning up after them. The tables were covered with lacy tablecloths, embroidered tablecloths, and mountainous platters of food. Fried chicken, fried fish, ham, roast beef, lamb stew with rice, fried calf's liver with onion gravy, baked sweet potatoes, scalloped potatoes, potato salad, macaroni and cheese, green pea salad, corn on the cob, collard greens, cabbage, candied carrots, turnip greens with turnips, black-eyed peas, crowder peas, lima beans, fried okra, gulf crawdads, yeast rolls, cornbread, yellow cake with chocolate icing, pound cakes, pies, puddings, homemade ice cream, and galvanized tubs of lemonade and iced tea. There was always a ton of food to be enjoyed by all. First by the white folks, and when they had eaten their fill and were sitting back with the ladies politely chattering amongst themselves, the men smoking or chawing tobacco, and the children playing, the blacks got to eat whatever was left over. This process of gorging, setting, and relaxing was a prelude to the next two church services that same Sunday. Sunday school ran from 3:00 p.m. to 5:00 p.m. There was an hour break, and then the evening worship service began at 6:00 p.m. and lasted sometimes until 8:30 or 9:00 p.m. The whites would ride home in their carriages, and the blacks would take the trek home, arriving in time to get to bed in preparation for work the next day.

On that day that has never been forgotten, church service had just ended, and the blacks were serving the whites the afternoon repast. Jeremiah, a fifteen-year-old slave, was serving a tray laden with iced tea to the table where the minister's family was seated. As he moved from the minister's wife to her sister with the iced tea, he accidentally lost his manners and flatulated loudly enough for everyone at the table to hear. He was embarrassed and hoped that no one had heard and, if they had, would not identify him as the culprit. James, who was serving the table next to him exclaimed loudly, "Ooh. He farted!" And then he started laughing. He abruptly stopped the laughter when he realized that he was the only one outwardly expressing amusement. The white folks pretended that they did not hear or smell anything, but they could be heard murmuring amongst themselves as they reentered the sanctuary for Sunday school.

"Humph! Folks ought to train their blacks on how to behave in public. Disgraceful!"

Now, Senhor Duartés was a proud white man. He considered himself to be his own self-made man. He had carved his own self plantation out of the woods in Newton, Mississippi. He took care of his own self family, ran his own self enterprise of logging and cotton, and he minded his own self business. There were only a few things that could make Senhor Duartés angry enough to betray the well-being of his own self blacks: lying, stealing, running away, sassing, and embarrassing him. Jeremiah and James had ultimately embarrassed him, and dammit, they had to be punished. Within an hour of arriving home and leading the family in the evening prayers, he had those two black boys taken to the barn and stripped naked. He made them lie down across bales of hay where he wailed against their naked flanks over and over again with a leather horse harness until every inch of their backs, buttocks and legs were covered with oozing welts or skin that had been split and was bleeding. Still oozing and barely able to walk, they were made to go to the fields the next day so that the other blacks could see what disobedience would garner them should they forget how they were expected to represent the Duartés plantation.

One hundred and ten years later, the Methodist church was still in the same place. It was now a black church. So much had happened since the Duartés days. The Civil War had come, Emancipation and then Reconstruction. Descendants of the first two blacks to arrive from the Bahamas banded together, worked, saved their money, and purchased the plantation, dropping the *s* from their names in the process. Hence, the land that was once owned by the white Duartés family became property of the black Duarté family. My father, Scripture Duarté, was the great-grandson of John, one of those first two arrivals on the plantation.

Black people drove to the church, some by buggy, a few by automobile; and on nice days, a few walked. Instead of being seated on the floor in front, everyone sat in a pew. Some pews were identified by brass name plates for the families that had made the monetary offering, and Scripture Duarté proudly sat in his own self family pew, right down at the front of the church. The afternoon repast was still a traditionally fine meal prepared the day before by the wives, mothers, sisters, and daughters of the men. It was served by the women to the men in the same splendor as had been served to the whites a century before, and the women retired to the sanctuary or under the trees to chat amongst themselves while the men smoked or chawed tobacco. The black children played as had the white children played. The difference now was that nearly everyone was black—the only exceptions being the white Methodist minister who was there on assignment along with his family.

The Sunday school service had been in process for about forty-five minutes when I, the second oldest of the boys, and Melody, the youngest of the Duarté children, simultaneously raised our right index fingers requesting permission to leave the sanctuary to relieve ourselves. There were covered outhouses to go to instead of bushes in the woods, and we could wash our hands with homemade lye soap and well water as opposed to creek water and laurel leaves. It was so refreshing outside! We did not want to go back inside to the hot humid sanctuary replete with the mixed odors of freshly pressed hair, aftershave, talcum powders, Jergens lotion, natural body musk, and a combination of colognes that would choke a horse. I convinced Melody to have Sunday school outside with me instead. We each searched the woods for long sticks and began our march through the vintage of graves, waving makeshift swords and singing "Onward, Christian Soldiers, Marching off to War!" Oh, we were having a ball until I dared to stomp on the actual graves instead of just marching down the aisles between them. The fifth grave I stomped on gave way, and my right leg went in up to my knee! I screamed, "Help me, Melody! Something dead got a hold of my leg." Terrified beyond her four years of life, Melody ran, stumbling into the sanctuary, pleading for assistance. "Help! Help! A dead man got Cleophus's leg and won't let it go!" The black folk in that church mobilized immediately and flew out of the sanctuary to save an eleven-year-old black boy who had been captured—maybe by the Klan, who were known to employ ghostly appearances to terrorize black people. When they saw me with my leg stuck in the grave, they were relieved. I was pulled out of the grave and turned over to Scripture Duarté, our father. As we all returned to the sanctuary, my father overheard several of the remarks deliberately made within his earshot: "Humph! Folks ought to train their chirren on how to behave in public. Disgraceful!"

Now, my father, Scripture Duarté, was a proud black man. He considered himself to be his own self-made man. His family had purchased the plantation their forebears had toiled on. It was all theirs now. He took care of his own self family, ran his own self farm, and minded his own self business. There were only a few things that could make Scripture Duarté angry enough to betray the well-being of his own children: lying, stealing, running away, sassing, and embarrassing him. Melody and I had ultimately embarrassed him, and dammit, we had to be punished.

That night after supper and prayers, he had us both taken to his bedroom and stripped down to our underwear. I pleaded for Melody and begged that I be given her whooping as well as my own. I was eleven years old, and Melody was only four. My father agreed because I was a man child. Men had the responsibility of making sure that the females in the family were taken care of and disciplined if need be. I had failed in my responsibility of making sure that Melody was safely back in the sanctuary—not marching around the graves like some hooligan. The punishment for Melody would be that she had to stand there and watch while he beat me, her favorite brother. My father made me lie down across his bed, and he beat me with a razor strap until every inch of my back, buttocks, and legs were covered with oozing welts or skin that had been split and was bleeding. I felt humiliated in front of my little sister, but at the same time, I felt proud that I had stood up for her and spared her the torture of our father's relentless strap. The following Sunday, my father made me wear short pants to church so that the church members could see the evidence of what disobedience would garner in the Duarté household. Humph, he showed them that he knew how to train his own self chirren on how to behave in public.

CHAPTER 3

Cleophus

DANG, IT WAS TAKING HER a long time. I had been waiting at the entrance of the woods for my little sister, Melody, who should be coming home from school. We had to walk nearly seven miles through the woods to get home, and Melody was not allowed to walk by herself. I had stopped attending school after the third grade because I was needed to help with the workload in the fields. At fourteen years of age, my only respite from the cotton fields came at three thirty each day when I was to meet Melody at the entrance of the woods and walk home with her. No child, especially a girl child, should walk those woods by herself. The dangers ranged from snakes, bears, wild dogs, and boars to deranged coon-hunting white men. An adult or strong youth could avoid the snakes and fend off the wild dogs, boars, and bears; and they could run and hide from the deranged coon-hunting white men. Girls and most women did not stand a chance even if they toted a rifle or a substantial blade with them. I had been taught by my father that my duty was to protect the womenfolk and the land at all costs, so I waited patiently to escort little Melody through the woods safely home.

The old Studebaker was heard and smelled before it was seen. Quite a rattletrap with bent hubcaps, the front hood tied down with a length of boat rope, and it emitted dark gray smoke from the tailpipe. This carnage of past vehicular splendor pulled up next to me.

The window rolled down and a raspy voice called out, "Hey, boy! You there! Come over here!"

I cautiously looked into the vehicle. There were two overstuffed white men in the front seat and an older, much thinner one in the back seat. All three appeared and smelled as if they were beyond the demarcation lines of unwashed body and sloppy drunkenness.

"What can I do for you, gentlemen?" I politely and waveringly asked.

"We be having a hard time understanding this map and these here woods. In other words, we be lost. Can you help us out? You live around here?"

I was not about to tell them where we lived, but I figured that I could help them out with the map as I did learn how to read and write before I left school. Mapping was something that I thoroughly enjoyed doing.

"Why, yessuh. I can help you with that map. Let me see it."

"Come closer, boy. I done already et, and I ain't about to bite you."

The white man sitting on the passenger side had the map sprawled out against his ample-sized abdomen.

"Stick your head in the window and show me where about we is so we can figure out how to get to where we should be going."

I felt that the quicker I could point out their direction, the quicker they would be on their way and away from where little Melody was scheduled to show up at any minute. I stuck my head in the passenger window so that I could get a closer look at the map. Laughing and showering me with stanky sprayed saliva, that man quickly rolled up the window on my neck, capturing me like prey.

"Hey, what are you doing to me?"

The driver gunned the motor, but the car would only creak slowly, allowing me to run alongside with my head engaged in the rolled-up window. I ran alongside of the vehicle, feeling the urine of panic run down my pant legs while keeping up with the momentum, knowing that a slip would have me dragged by my neck to my death. I stopped pleading with the perpetrators to let me go and just kept up with that old Studebaker as it drove further into the woods.

I felt that my death might come at any time, but at least I had protected my little sister Melody from whatever treachery could have befallen her. About a mile into the woods, they decided to let me go. I wasn't hollering like the last nigra they had strangled in this fashion. I wasn't any fun, so they just stopped the car, rolled down the window, pushed me out onto the earth, and clambered away farting, spitting, and laughing about their exploit.

When I felt my body hit the earth, I finally relaxed and passed out. I must have slept for three or four hours because it was dark when I woke up. I ran to the fork in case Melody might still be there. She was not. I ran the seven miles through the woods home, praying that the scumbags did not encounter my little sister all alone in the woods. When I got home, everything was quiet. My father, Scripture, was waiting in the parlor for me. When my father saw the condition that I was in, he reached out to embrace me, listened to my story, and then checked my body all over for broken bones. Good. There were none. He prayed forcefully that night and thanked the Lord for bringing me safely home from my ordeal. My mother was called to bathe me and fix me something to eat. Then I was put to bed.

I was still in the midst of a pleasant dream early the next morning when I was awakened by my father, who explained to me that I was about to get a whooping. Melody had walked through the woods alone the night before. My job was to protect her, and I had failed and would need to be punished. What those white men had done to me was terrible, but the story could have had a different deadly ending. What I should have done was to use my head and my wits. When I heard and smelled that vehicle coming, I should have hidden until it passed. Then I could have safely met little Melody and escorted her home through those seven miles of woods. I had not used the brains and common sense that the Lord had given me.

"Your soul belongs to the Lord, but right now, your backside belongs to me. You will never make this type of mistake again."

My father then thoroughly whooped me, his own self son, soundly to make sure that the lesson would take hold. It did.

CHAPTER 4

Cleophus

MY FATHER, SCRIPTURE DUARTÉ, RAN his home like a military camp. He had to. He had the responsibility of maintaining the family home and all who resided within. Everybody had a job to do, and there was no toleration for a slacker. He was a man of few words, but he wielded a mighty arm that he would use to quell insolence or disobedience. He would firmly slap my mother across her face for defying him, and he would beat the living daylights out of anyone of his offspring who dared to not listen and break his rules. We, the children, saw it as pure and utter meanness, but my father saw it as a survival mechanism. When a child was late coming home, immediate steps had to be taken in case a life was in danger. Those searching for the child placed their own lives in danger should they be found by a group of Klansmen out looking for some evening fun. A colored man or even two colored men in the woods could easily fall prey to a group of Klansmen out for an evening of recreational "coon hunting." Last winter, Jasper Bohannon had been found hanging in a tree, castrated. He had ventured into the woods at night to look for his hunting dog that had not come home. That night, Jasper did not come home either. So my father would firmly discipline any child of his who came home late.

My father made sure that there was always enough food available for his family. He allowed my mother to kill only so many chickens per week. She could open only so many jars of preserves per month. The flour, sugar, coffee, salt, and cornmeal had to last until he said that more could be obtained at the general store. My mother made her own lye soap, butter, and cheese. She was allowed to fry only so many eggs for the Sunday morning breakfast, and those siblings who went to school were allowed to only take one nut butter and applesauce sandwich with them. My father was determined that his family would not experience hunger. He was also determined that his family would not run up an outrageous bill at the general store by restocking supplies that they had wasted. He saw the general store as an open invitation to legal enslavement. Those who ran up bills and were unable to pay them were conscripted into the county jail system, where they served their time clearing roads and cutting down trees. Many an innocent colored man had found such a fate. No! He wasn't going to have any of that. If everyone followed his rules, they would have all that they needed. Is it any wonder that he firmly disciplined those who transgressed from his policies?

My father ran a Saturday afternoon Bible study for the young colored children of the area. Around about 12:30 p.m., he would appear at the church, ring the bell, and call out, "Bible study! Bible study!" Children would already be en route to the church, and they would hasten their steps to get there in time for the snacks my mother, whom they called Sister Arnetta, prepared for them. The snacks were usually tea cakes, warm chewy vanilla cookies still warm from my mother's oven. Each child would get just one if they were there on time (1:00 p.m.), and then the Bible study lesson would commence. My father had spent the night before developing his lesson for the children. It was to focus on Moses and the Hebrews traveling through the dessert during their exodus from Egypt. Today, he was going to share information about the time that they were starving in the desert and God had blessed them with water from a rock and manna from heaven. My mother had offered to make extra smaller cookies that they could pretend was manna from heaven, but he said, "No, we are not going to waste any unnecessary eggs, butter, flour, and sugar." He was unpleasantly surprised to find an extra satchel of those smaller cookies in the basket when he opened it up. My mother was unpleasantly surprised when he nearly slapped her head sideways when he got home that afternoon. He didn't say much to her. He just walked into the kitchen, placed the basket down on the table, and nearly took her head off! My mother had learned not to cry out when he slapped her because it would bring the children running to see what was going on. She never wanted the children to actually see him hit her because she never wanted them to feel that they had to do something. She had heard stories of teenaged boys who had taken shotguns to their own fathers for such repeated transgressions. Instead, she turned her anger and her fear inwards. She was able to expel that pent-up anger, frustration, and pain the following week.

It was Saturday, and she and my father had gone to Miz Wheeler's place to sit with her. Miz Wheeler's husband had just died from a stroke, and the tradition was to sit with the widow all day and through the night until the body was buried the following morning. We thought that our parents would be gone for a long time, and we decided that we wanted to eat something other than the meal of day-old cornbread and pinto beans left for our supper. We wanted fried chicken, biscuits, and gravy. Brother, the eldest boy, had the job of cutting the chicken's head off. He marveled at the power that surged through his body when the hapless chicken was flopping headless against the fence, so he killed a second chicken. I had the job of gutting the birds while the six youngest ones had the task of pulling off all the feathers. Sister, the eldest girl, fried up the two chickens, made biscuits and gravy, and rationed out the chicken pieces. The backs were fried, pulled apart, and used to season the gravy. Everyone got a big piece and a small piece except for Brother and me, who got a breast section, a wing, and a neck apiece. Sister and Viney got a breast section and a wing apiece, while four of the smaller children each received a drumstick and a thigh apiece. The only exception was Scrip Jr., the youngest boy. He had made a pet of a baby chick last spring, and he had raised her to full growth, lovingly naming her Miz Clacky. When Mommie killed Miz Clacky and fried her up for dinner one Sunday, Scrip had a crying fit and refused to eat chicken from that day forward. Hence, we didn't have to give him a piece of our fried chicken bounty that night. Scrip was satisfied with biscuits, gravy, pinto beans, and cornbread. After we had dined to our pleasure, we took care to clean up the kitchen and yard well. There must be no evidence of our treachery anywhere.

Our parents came home earlier than expected. We had assumed that they would be out until after the funeral the next day, but they came home that night instead. They walked into the kitchen, and our mother immediately went out to her hen house to count. She came back inside and asked one question, "Which one of y'all killed my chickens?" She didn't even wait for an answer. She picked up a piece of two-by-four that she used to stir the fire with, and she began slamming each of us children about the head and shoulders. She didn't have to say anything. She used her pent-up energy and anger and whooped the hell out of us—all nine of us. We would know better than to mess with her chickens again. We had used up a day's portion of flour and cooking oil to boot! She had to beat us so that our father would not beat her! We wondered, "How did she know?" It was years later when we realized that you can wash and dry dishes, mop the floor, take the scraps out to the hogs, but there is no way to chase out the mouthwatering smell of freshly fried chicken. Our mother knew as soon as she walked into the house what we had done, and we paid the price for our misdeed.

CHAPTER 5

Cleophus

WIEGLER LUMBER COMPANY WAS HIRING! Wiegler was the premier lumber company in Newton, Mississippi, and the largest employer in the county. Wiegler sold construction grade wood—red pine, southern yellow pine, and a mixture of spruce, pine, and fir called SPF. I was determined to get myself a good job there. Unlike many of the colored and white laborers who were employed there, I could read, write, and do arithmetic in my head—accurately. Most of the colored laborers worked as loggers, dock crew, or janitors. They cleaned up the sawdust in the mill, or if they worked outside, they loaded freshly cut logs in the woods, or they loaded freshly cut planks onto trucks, trains or boats for shipment. In either case, they were always paid less than their white counterparts. For example, the colored clean-up men were called janitors. The white clean-up men were call industrial maintenance workers, and they were paid more for doing the same work.

I had left school after the third grade to help to bring in the money needed to keep the family land out of the hands of the unscrupulous whites who were not fond of colored people who owned their own property. There were numerous attempts to get at the Duarté land: missing documentation of taxes paid, overcharging at the general store, inventing fines layered upon my father for walking on the wrong side of the road. Once, he was fined because his horse defecated in the road that leads to town. In each case, my father just repaid the taxes or paid the trumped-up fine, wished the sheriff a blessed day, and then went on about his business. My mother, the boys, and the two eldest girls were counted upon to help keep the family land in the family; thus, we children had to go to work early. The property taxes amounted to about $52 per year, and the "fines" tended to be an amount that ranged from $50 to $250 each. Hence, my father made it a practice to keep a minimum of $1,000 cash secreted someplace on his property so that he could get to it at a moment's notice. He taught his sons that to be a man, we had to have our own self property, be able to feed and house our family, and we each needed to have a minimum of $1,000 available at any given time for white folk–designed emergencies.

I had started off my money-making enterprise by selling slices of Sister's cake to the men working in the woods, felling and trimming trees. Sister made the best pound cake in the county. She baked, cleaned house, and did laundry for Miz Baxter, the meanest white lady in the county. When she baked her prize-winning pound cakes for Miz Baxter each week, she baked additional ones for her family. Miz Baxter considered her donation of eggs, butter, sugar, and flour as part of the weekly salary that Sister was to receive. Sister averaged bringing home four cakes per week. The family shared one of those cakes during the Sunday dinner, and the other three cakes were sliced, wrapped in waxed paper, and carted off to the working area in the woods, where I sold them for five cents a slice, or I bartered them for something else like a cigarette. Hence, I started smoking at the age of nine unbeknownst to my parents. I learned how to chew the leaves of a bay laurel tree to cleanse my breath of the smell of tobacco, and I kept a handful of those leaves in my pocket for that very purpose. Half of my earnings I gave to my father. I put five cents in the Sunday school offering plate and five cents in the mission offering plate each Sunday. The mission offering was supposed to support poor starving people in India. I had a hard time understanding why poor starving colored people in Mississippi were dutifully concerned about sending money to poor starving people in another country, but I knew better than to ask my father, who served as one of the church deacons. After expenses, I sometimes cleared anywhere from $1.50 to $2.00 a week from my pound cake enterprise, and I saved every penny of it in a series of old coffee cans that I kept buried adjacent to a magnolia tree on the north side of the pig pen. As I reached $100 in a coffee can, I buried it in a grave bank. Each grave bank was eighteen inches deep and twenty-seven inches from the outside of the magnolia tree with the first a direct line from the burn mark I had placed in the bark with a lit cigarette. After that, they were twenty-four clockwise inches apart. The pigs kept up a ruckus whenever anyone came near that pig pen, so I had a built-in alarm system to protect my stash of cash.

At the age of sixteen, I was ready to take on a man's challenge and do real man's work. I was going to apply for a job at the mill. Most of the colored boys my age had stopped their schooling around the same time that I did to go to work. The jobs available to us were butchering hogs, picking cotton, picking chickens, gardening in the white folks' part of town, sweeping the streets, and digging sweet potatoes. No, I wanted a real man's job in the Wiegler Lumber Mill. I could read, write, and do arithmetic as good as any white man my age. I had seen the announcement for the job openings, and I had carefully copied it down. I looked at it now and pointed my right index finger to each position as I read: truck driver, industrial maintenance, assistant plant manager, procurement manager, general labor, accountant, and general office clerk. Hmm, the only one I could not do was drive the truck because I did not have a license. I knew that industrial maintenance referred to the white janitorial team. I would have to work my way up to being one of the managers. General labor meant cutting down trees, trimming trees, and loading—dangerous work. I knew that I could do the accountant job and I could do the general office clerk job as well.

When I went into the human resources office of the Wiegler Lumber Mill to submit my application, I saw that there were two lines of men—one white line and one colored line. I took my place in the colored line and waited patiently. I observed that there were some young white males about my own age in the white line, and someone from the office was helping them to fill out their applications. It was obvious that these boys could not read and write because the questions that I heard asked of them were the same questions that were on the application: name, address, date of birth, religion, marital status, children, general health, vision problems, ability to lift fifty pounds, etc. Most of the colored men just signed an X at the bottom of the application, leaving the clerk to put whatever he felt was needed on the rest of the application.

"Who filled this out for you, boy?" the clerk had asked when I showed him that I had a completed application.

"I filled it out and signed it for myself, suh," I had answered.

"You from round heah?"

"Yessuh. I am one of Scripture Duartés's sons, and we live in the southeast section of the Newton Woods."

"Most of the nigras that come in here don't have enough schoolin' to fill out this application without help, and now here you are. Who in the hell do you think you is?"

"Suh, I don't want no trouble, I just want to work to help feed my family."

I was hired on that day in the industrial maintenance section of warehouse #3. My job with all my skills in reading, writing, and the ability to do arithmetic in my head accurately consisted of sweeping up the piles of sawdust that accumulated on an ongoing basis. It was not what I was anticipating, but it was a paying job. My plan was to learn everything thing about the lumber business that I could from the bottom to the top, and then be the first Negro lumber entrepreneur in the state of Mississippi! I would be a millionaire before I was thirty years of age!

The white boys about my own age that I had observed being helped with their applications were assigned to better-paying positions, and that is where they would stay during their tenure of employment with the Wiegler Lumber Company—just like their fathers, uncles, brothers, and cousins. Some of them were in warehouse #3, and they learned how to operate the machinery that would cut the logs into planks. John Paul was one of those white boys who were about the same age as me. I would watch John Paul as he received instructions from one of the journeymen on how to operate the equipment. Humph! I should be the one doing that work. John

Paul didn't have enough sense to pour piss out of a boot with the directions printed on the heel, much less calculate the measurement of the wood that he was assigned to cut. When no one was observing, I would help John Paul out by setting the lathe to the proper dimensions, and I myself would guide John Paul's hands as he placed the wood on the table to be cut. I thought that we had developed a kinship that would one day help me to get on in the same line of work. I would develop kinship relationships with other white boys along the way if it would get me to where I ultimately wanted to be. I took to packing an extra slice of cake for John Paul's lunch, and I would give him free cigarettes. The other colored men told me that I was crazy to befriend one of the white boys.

"Fool! Don't you know that if he is ever confronted by one of the white men, he will turn on you quicker than a cat can lick its own behind with its tongue already poised at the hole!"

"Naw, he is just a plain ole southern boy, just like me. It ain't his fault that the owners treat the colored workers differently. Things will change, and I am gonna be in position to take advantage of the change when it comes."

On a muggy Thursday afternoon, John Paul and I were observed by the journeyman talking and working together on the scythe. John Paul was disillusioned and confused about some new equipment, and I was explaining to him how to calculate the measurements and execute the cuts safely.

"Hey, boy! What in the hell you doing over there! John Paul, what in the hell are you doing over there with him? You know that nigras ain't allowed to touch that equipment!"

John Paul just shook his shoulders and said, "I don't know. He was standing here when I come in."

John Paul turned to me, spat on the floor, and snarled, "Nigger, get the shits back to sweeping that floor and get the hell away from me. This here is my position!"

The following Thursday, John Paul miscalculated the length of a log that he was working on and cut off his left hand while tendering the machinery. While the young illiterate yet privileged white boy was rushed off to the medic, bleeding profusely and yowling in pain, I, the nigger who could read, write, and do arithmetic accurately in my head, carefully dropped fresh sawdust on the bloodstains, swept them up, deposited it all into the rubbish, and then went on about my own self business of keeping the warehouse floors clear.

CHAPTER 6

Cleophus

"Boil the ham hocks on a low fire all morning long. That gets the flavor and salts into the water before you split it between the two pots—one for beans and the other for greens. Now, to make good greens, you need to put in just a pinch of baking soda into the pot. Helps to cut down on the gas. You make the cornbread last. Use your hand to measure out the cornmeal and then the flour. Add that little blue cup full of sugar, that yellow cup full of milk, a fingertip of salt, a spoon of baking powder, and then pour in some bacon drippings."

"How much baking drippings?" Viney asked.

"As much as you need, that's how much. Damn, girl, don't you remember nothin'? I been telling you all month long how to make cornbread, and you ain't learnt a thing. I got to go so's I won't be late. Miz Baxter is having a High Tea for the uppity white ladies tomorrow, and she needs me to wash, starch, and iron those old musty linens that she keeps in a chest in the attic."

Sister, the oldest girl, was instructing Viney, the sister next in age to her, on how to start the dinner. With Mommie and Daddy both working all day, the eldest girls had the responsibility of running the home until they returned. Running the home entailed gathering eggs and milk in the morning, feeding the chickens, getting the breakfast out, getting the youngest off to school with their lunch sacks, and having the evening meal hot and ready when Mommie and Daddy returned. All this, and Sister also had a job working at the Baxter Place. She routinely cleaned floors, dusted shelves, polished silver, beat rugs, washed dishes, washed and ironed clothes, and baked for Miz Baxter. On special occasions, Miz Baxter called on her to do special things. A very special occasion was coming up. Miz Baxter had invited the gentlewomen of Newton to her home for *High Tea*, and she wanted to impress them with what had once been the finery of the Baxter Family Plantation. The home had to be spotless and shining. The table linens had to be specially ironed and creased at the appropriate places. The lace table doilies had to be starched and ironed so that they stood up at attention. Miz Baxter had read somewhere that the British High Tea contained no less than fourteen menu items, so she designed her menu as she imagined the proper British woman of means would. She would show the fine ladies of Newton who she was!

The High Tea Menu had been decided weeks ago:

Scones with lemon curd and Devonshire cream
Sister's Famous Lemon Tea Cakes

Seven different kinds of Tea Sandwiches
Deviled Ham
Egg Salad
Sliced Beef with Creamy Horseradish
Watercress with Cucumber
Curried Chicken
Salmon with Goat Cheese and Parsley
Olive and Mushroom

Five different kinds of Savories
Swedish Meatballs
Creamy Chicken Popovers
Gulf Shrimp Cups
Crab Cakes
Quiche Lorraine

Four different kinds of Crudités
Tossed Green Salad
Roasted Beets and Bell Peppers
Cherry Tomatoes stuffed with Cream Cheese
Fruit Salad

Three different kinds of Desserts
Sister's Famous Golden Pound Cake
Fresh Peaches
Vanilla Bean Ice Cream

Beverages
Hot Coffee and Tea
Iced Tea with Lemon and Mint
Strawberry Lemonade

Miz Baxter had hired extra cooks to make the preparations. Her sisters, first cousins, and her husband's aunts, sisters, and first cousins were coming in from Meridian and Jackson. Oh, it was to be the affair of the year! Everything had to be just perfect! Sister planned to reach Miz Baxter's place by 7:00 a.m. so that she would have the time to do what she needed to do. First, she would wash the linens and doilies and get them all on the line by 8:00 a.m. That way, they could dry in the sun for several hours while she baked the tea cakes and pound cakes and sliced up and seasoned the peaches with brown sugar and brandy. After she had cleaned up the kitchen, she could spend the afternoon starching and ironing the linens and doilies. She could have them all set up on the inside tables before she left that night. She would come over early the next morning and set up the outside tables with their linens and then place the floral centerpieces, fine china, and flatware in place.

Sister was on her way to the front door when the first wave of nausea hit her. Oh no! Not today! She took deep breaths, tried to ignore the pain in her chest, and went back into the kitchen to sit for a minute and get a cool drink of water. She just had time to bolt out of the backdoor before she started coughing violently and regurgitating repeatedly. Viney followed her outside, touched Sister's face, and quickly snatched her hand back.

"Girl, you as hot as a biscuit just come out of the oven! Does your chest hurt when you take breaths?"

Sister shook her head up and down, indicating the answer to that question was yes. "It hurts the worst when I breathe in," she whispered.

"Darn, girl, you got the pleurisy!" exclaimed Viney. "It was going around the Harper place, the Overton place and the Higgins place last week, and now you got it! You ain't about to go no place today but in the bed. I'll make you some sassafras tea with honey for right now. It will help to settle your stomach. Then I will bring you some broth and crackers later. When Mommie and Daddy get home, I will tell them, and Daddy can go to town to get you some of that new medicine called penicillin. All you can do with pleurisy is wait it out, and try not to give it to the rest of us!"

Viney sent word to our parents regarding Sister's affliction, and Mommie came home almost immediately. She stopped first at the school house to get Melody. Melody would have to get over to Miz Baxter's place to do Sister's job of preparing for the High Tea the next day.

It was a disgruntled Melody, barely turned ten, who showed up at the Baxter Place around 11:00 a.m. Miz Baxter was beside herself. She had been expecting Sister since early that morning, and now here was this short-haired pickaninny!

"You are not Sister! What do you think that you can do?"

"Sister is sick, so I am all you got for today. Where do you want me to start?"

Miz Baxter stomped her foot on the floor, realized that she was caught in a bind, and then relented.

"You need to get the linens and doilies out of the chest in the attic, wash them, starch them, dry and iron them. Do you think you can muster up enough smarts to do that?"

"Would you rather I do something else?"

"You have a smart-assed mouth, little girl. You would do well to just do as you are told and keep the smart-ass comments to yourself. You just might live longer."

"So might you," Melody whispered as she made her way up to the attic. Ugh! The dank and musty smell of that attic made her want to turn around and run home, but Mommie had told her to take up where Sister had left off and finish the job. So she dragged the linens downstairs, bleached and washed them, rinsed them twice, and then she hung them out on the line to dry. She was already four hours late getting started on this task because her day had initially started at school, a place where she wished she was now. It was after 1:00 p.m., and had she still been in school, she would be in the middle of her geography lesson, a subject she loved and excelled in. Normally, Sister would have let the linens dry on the line for about five hours and then taken them in for ironing. Melody began to calculate her time, knowing that she needed to be through with her work in time to walk through the woods to get home before dusk. It was not safe to be alone in the woods after dusk.

Melody pulled the linens off the clothesline around 3:00 p.m., and they were not completely dry. She determined that she would finish the drying process with the ironing. She had just finished what she determined was a fairly decent job with the linens when Miz Baxter came in to inspect her work.

"Girl, what in the black-assed hell did you do? These linens are not crisp the way that Sister does them, and where are my doilies?"

"Miz Baxter, I didn't have time to do the doilies and the linens, so I just did the linens, and they are ironed well. I don't know what you are complaining about."

"You impudent little nappy-headed bitch! You take those linens and do them over, and I want them to be as sharp and as crisply ironed as if Sister ironed them herself! And you are not to leave here until it is done. I don't care if it takes you all night! And I want my doilies as well! Do you understand me? Can't trust a nigra to do anything right!"

Melody stomped her foot on the wooden floor, completely startling Miz Baxter, and yelled, "My momma didn't give birth to no dogs, so I am not a bitch. You want 'em done over? Do 'em your damn self!"

She took off out of the backdoor, down the steps, down the road, and into the woods, hearing a frantic Miz Baxter lamenting, "You just wait! I am going to tell my husband about you! You just wait!"

Melody made it home just before dusk. She sat down at the kitchen table and rested while Viney was finishing up the supper.

"How did it go today?" Viney had asked her.

"I hope I never have to go to work for that woman ever again. She yelled at me, stomped her foot at me, and she called me an impudent little nappy-headed bitch. The nerve of her. I wanted to pop her upside her head and gouge her eyes out!"

"You just ain't used to workin' for white folks. You have to not let them get under your skin like that. You do your work, and you get paid. You don't let the mean things they say to and about you get to you. They gonna get theirs, and it don't have to be you who gives it to 'em."

I came in along with Brother and Andrew. "Mommie and Daddy are going to be late, so we are to go ahead and have our supper."

Ivey, the third oldest sister, had come down from Sister's room, so we all joined hands to give thanks for the meal, then we sat down to eat.

We heard the truck before it came to a screeching halt in front of the house. There was no time to go to the door to look out to determine who it was coming by at night like that. Mr. Baxter stormed up the steps to the porch, kicked open the door, and lumbered into the hallway.

"Whar is she?" he bellowed. "Whar is that damn black-assed pickaninny who sassed my wife today?"

Everyone stood frozen. Mr. Baxter was only about five feet four inches tall, but he made up for his lack of stature with a loaded shotgun that he menacingly brandished in his right hand. He stomped over to Melody and slapped her across the face with his left hand so hard that she flipped over her chair and landed on the floor at Brother's feet.

"Now, you hold on there. You ain't got no cause to be hittin' on my baby sister. You ain't got no cause!"

Our father had taught us boys that it was our job to protect the women of the family, and this is what Brother was trying to do. Brother ran up to Mr. Baxter and pushed him back up against the wall. Mr. Baxter raised that shotgun, leveled it at Brother, and shot him square in the chest; and he appeared to be reloading his shotgun again. Enraged, I then sprang at Mr. Baxter, took the shotgun from him, hit him in the jaw with the butt, and then fired squarely into his chest! Our parents came home that evening to a house replete with screaming and sobbing daughters, their eldest son dead, Mr. Baxter dead, with me, Andrew, and Scrip Jr. trying to clean up the blood. The story we told was that Mr. Baxter had shot Brother, and Brother had managed to take the shotgun away and shoot Mr. Baxter before succumbing to his own mortal wounds. A twelve-gauge shotgun leaves quite the hole at the entry point and rips bone, flesh, and just about everything else away at the exit point. There was no way that Brother could have survived long enough to do what we said. The fingers would point to the next son in line, me. I had to leave, and I had to leave right away. The penalty for killing a white man in Mississippi was a horrible death—even if the white man had killed the perpetrator's brother first. I left that night with just the clothes on my back, two of the cans of cash that I had buried, a biscuit with bacon, and an apple wrapped into a kerchief as I was hidden under a load of freshly cut wood plank from the Wiegler Lumber Company that was traveling by truck to Meridian. I was just seventeen years of age, and the life I once knew was behind me. A new life was ahead.

Chapter 7

Cleophus

I HID OUT ON THE banks of the Sowashee Creek in Meridian. I blended well into the scenery of homeless people who lived off what they could catch and sell from the creek and what they could forage in the wooded areas. I made a friend, Stuart, who became sort of my guardian angel. He was thin, pitch black, about six feet tall, and he had some of that good wavy hair. He said that he was from down Nacogdochesway and was working to get himself up north, where there were better opportunities for a colored man. It was Stuart who had taught me that it was safer to sleep tied up in a tree as opposed to on the banks of the creek. Folks who slept on the banks of the creek faced the danger of being bitten by a muskrat, snake, or alligator. Some of the folks kept soonas around that would bark a warning when some critter came too close. Stuart and I could have safely slept on the banks of the creek, but we would have had to share whatever food we had with the soonas. I doubled up with laughter when Stuart explained to me why those dogs were called soonas.

"He is a low-down trashy mutt dog. Don't belong to nobody. Eats whatever it can. In fact, he will soon as eat his own shit as anything else that he can find."

We made plans to leave when colored babies began to disappear from the homeless camps. Rumor had it that the babies were taken to be used as live bait by white alligator hunters. Stuart and I decided that we did not need to be involved with the vengeful killing of white

35

men, so we readily changed venues. I wondered if there was a secret killing somewhere in Stuart's past, but I did not ask him. If there was a secret, it was his own self business.

We two men heard that there were good jobs available at the Okatibbee Water Park. Men were needed to steer the boats of white pleasure fishermen, help them bait their lines, and clean their catches. Because of my youth, most of my work involved baiting the lines, hauling in the catches, and cleaning them. Those white men caught bream, bluegill, catfish, largemouth bass, crappie, white bass, bowfin, blue catfish, brown trout, and perch. I learned to be real careful when I helped them land the catfish and even more careful when I cleaned them. Damn! I started bringing a pair of pliers with me to use to pull off the catfish skin, being very careful to avoid those barbs. They could stab just like sharp pointed darning needles. These pleasure fishermen did not always want to take their catches home, and they never wanted the perch. Stuart and I had a sideline business going every evening after we brought the boat back in. We sold fresh fish fillets to two white restaurants located along the pier. Whatever the white restaurants did not want, we sold to Almary Jenkins, who owned and operated a colored juke joint.

We spent nearly every evening at Almary's place, where we could eat, drink, gamble, dance, and check out the foxy women who frequented the place. Hell, we were making good money and living well, but we had to leave the area when some man's wife was found straddling my lap with her lips curled around the edge of a mason jar filled with a regional drink called "strip and go naked." This potent drink was mixed in a galvanized bathtub and consisted of slow gin, beer, vodka, lemons, sugar, and ice. You had two mason jars of that concoction, and you were ready to "strip and go naked" on the spot of consumption. The woman's husband walked in and saw her voraciously squirming on my lap, and he had charged toward me with an ice pick in his hand aimed for my back. Only Stuart had pulled me aside, and the ice pick had plunged into the chest of his wife instead. Pandemonium broke out! Chairs, bottles, plates, fists, and bricks were thrown with reckless abandon. The music of the piano and the guitar picked up with the fervor of the melee. Then someone shouted, "He's got a gun!" That juke joint emptied quickly. Folks were scurrying out of windows and doors as deftly as cockroaches scurry when the lights come on. Knowing already about how vengeful a jilted man can be, Stuart and I did not even bother to go home. We took off that night.

We briefly took work loading on the docks of the Chickasawhay River and eventually made our way east to Birmingham, Alabama, where we both enlisted in the United States Air Force. The first time we tried to enlist, we both were turned down and advised to try the Army. The Army did not require a high school diploma, whereas the United States Air Force did. Not to be defeated, I tutored Stuart for the GED exam while I studied for it myself. We both passed and were enlisted into the USAF. Like most of the colored country boys aiming to escape life as a share cropper, Stuart was content to be an enlisted man with a salary, benefits, a place to sleep, food, and the opportunity to travel all around the world. I, on the other hand, had other aspirations. The United States Air Force was going to be my career. I was going to make it all the way to the top! Or so I thought at that time.

CHAPTER 8

Cleophus

STUART AND I WERE BOTH stationed at the Maxwell Air Force Base in Montgomery, Alabama—right in the heart of Jim Crow. Some of the same racist white boys who would hang a Negro in the south ended up either enlisting or being drafted into the services. The racial hatred did not disguise itself on base. We colored did not go into the latrine when the white boys were in there because it was not unheard of to be pissed on by one or more of them. I had to put up with being spat on, tripped, and called nigger over and over again. I could not physically respond because those colored men who did respond in public with their fists found themselves in the brig and in some cases dishonorably discharged or blue-ticketed from the service. A blue ticket discharge was as bad as a felony conviction. You could not find a job because no one would hire you, and you were legally denied GI benefits.

In those days, the colored and the white servicemen did not eat, drink, or gamble at the same tables. Only a privileged few were allowed to work in the offices as opposed to the kitchen or on janitorial detail. The few who had the talent took up boxing and used their skills to legitimately beat the hell out of white boy contestants.

On July 26, 1948, President Harry S. Truman signed Executive Order 9981 integrating the military and mandating equality of treatment and opportunity. It also made it illegal, per military law, to make a racist remark. The integration commanded by Truman's 1948

Executive Order extended to schools and neighborhoods as well as military units. Fifteen years after the executive order, Secretary of Defense Robert McNamara issued Department of Defense Directive 5120.36.

"Every military commander," the directive mandates, "has the responsibility to oppose discriminatory practices affecting his men and their dependents and to foster equal opportunity for them, not only in areas under his immediate control, but also in nearby communities where they may gather in off-duty hours."

The base was integrated, on paper, but the separation of the colored and white was as evident in 1948 as it had been in 1938. Sure, we all ate in the same mess hall, but the colored ate in their area, usually at the back, the front or on the sides; and the whites ate in the central area. The central area was the ideal area. The lighting was better there. In the winter, that area was warmer because it was not adjacent to the windows, and it was the last area to receive the onslaught of the giant flying bugs that covered the ceilings. Those damned bugs fed like they were on a military stopwatch. The ceiling would be a muddy color when we first entered the mess hall. Toward the end of mess, those fat bugs, some up to two inches in length, would start to drop onto the tables at the perimeter—the ones where the colored men ate. They made a special landing sound when they hit the table—*plip!* You would hear them, and then you would see them racing for whatever crumbs or scraps of food were left on the tables and sometimes on someone's plate. *Plip! Plip! Plip! Plip! Plip! Plip plip! Plip plip plip! Plip plip plip plip plip plip plip plip plip!*

Some of the men called them water bugs, and some others called them Palmetto bugs. I knew the critters as flying cockroaches! The *plip* of the cockroaches was the signal for the colored to get up and get out of the mess hall before the offensive creatures fell onto their heads and down the backs of their clothing. The departure of the colored was the signal for the whites to get up and get out of the mess hall. Within five minutes of the first *plip*, the ceilings were back to their original dull green shade, and the tables and floor were teeming with the movement of hungry crawling cockroaches! Those damned things were in the latrine as well. We learned not to go into the latrine at night to relieve the bowels—only to use the urinals. Sitting down on a commode might warrant a bite on the butt from a large cockroach that did not appreciate being disturbed during its nocturnal adventures.

Gambling was a favorite pastime on base. I used my mathematical skills and earned quite a pretty penny from both races when they lost bets. As the base money lender, I loaned cash to enable white and colored enlisted and officers alike make it until the next payday. I would set up a folding card table right outside of the pay station on payday to make it convenient for those who owed to be able to pay. Any fool, white or colored, who thought he could get around paying me was quickly taught an important lesson, "Don't mess with Duarté and his money." One white officer who had suffered a run of bad luck and found it necessary to get bailed out by me had made the mistake of proclaiming on payday that he wasn't going to give no nigger his hard-earned pay. He was found later that same evening alive but with his skull neatly cracked open. A government-issued claw hammer was lying next to him. Stuart had advised me to wipe off my fingerprints and then leave it there as a message to anyone else who might feel the urge to challenge me regarding my money. That white officer never reported who had assaulted him, and he never forgot to "pay up" his gambling debts again. Because of the financial relationship that had developed between me and several of the higher level white officers, no charges were ever filed against anyone.

The first time I saw her, I knew that she would be my wife and the mother of my own self son. I didn't want a slew of kids like Mommie and Daddy had back in Newton, Mississippi. All I wanted was my own self son whom I would name Junior. I would raise that boy to be more of a genius than me. My son would be a scientist, a mathematician, a physicist. The world would be my son's oyster. Junior Duarté would be a well-educated Negro man of means, living high on the hog in the United States of America! His aspirations would be realized far beyond the world of just getting out of the south by singing, dancing, playing an instrument, or playing ball. His vehicle to success would be his brains and cunning, along with the opportunities that I, his father, would develop and provide for him. I had used my own intellect to pass the GED and earn a high school diploma, escape the life of a Mississippi farmer or low-esteemed laborer, and enter the Air Force. I had to be a cunning fighter every step of the way. The first time I took the test for advancement, I scored higher than any of the white boys. They claimed that I must have cheated, and I had to take the test over with a special proctor. I scored even higher the second time. Subsequent tests were met without challenge, and I worked my way up to E6 (technical sergeant) status. Using my own self brain, I would teach my own self son how to use the intellectual resources that God had blessed him with, and Aurora was the perfect vessel to house my future offspring.

Aurora was about five feet three inches tall, yellow, shapely, and she had long thick hair that needed to be straightened with a pressing comb. I believed that light-skinned women with "good hair" were a curse and brought damnation into the marital union because most colored men were attracted to colored women with hair that did not need to be straightened. I had done my investigative homework. I already knew that Aurora had been to a Teachers College in Virginia and had married Doc Henry and moved to Hamilton Field Air Force Base in Northern California with their son. Yes, she was a married woman, and she and her husband already had their own son. I first saw her in line at the commissary taking items off the belt because she did not have enough money to pay for all her choices. I began to keep mental notes. Hmm. She was light-skinned, had long nappy hair, was pretty, educated, and well-traveled. Her five-year-old son was healthy, well fed, well mannered, and well groomed. I figured that I could make a difference in her son's life by teaching him how to matriculate through life as a brilliant and successful Negro man— almost as brilliant and successful as my own self son was going to be. Yes, Aurora was good stock, and I felt that I could work with her to achieve my dreams.

I had shared my thoughts regarding Aurora with Stuart, and we both agreed that it would take a dedicated plan to win these treasures away from Doc Henry, and by the third time that I had seen her at the commissary, I knew exactly how the mission would be accomplished. Yes, I knew Doc Henry, and I knew about Doc Henry. We were both colored men in the white man's Air Force stationed on the same base in the San Francisco Bay Area. We both smoked filterless Pall Mall cigarettes, and we both lived in the section of the base relegated to the colored servicemen and their families. We both were from the south, me from Mississippi and Doc Henry from Virginia. We both drank Lucky Lager beer, and we both loved to gamble. It didn't matter if the game was billiards or poker, I routinely won, and Doc Henry routinely lost. I knew that when Doc Henry got snockered with the beer, he would bet more and consequently, lose more.

To put my plan in motion, I started to ply Doc Henry with unlimited amounts of free beer on those Friday nights, then I would challenge Doc Henry or arrange for someone else to present the challenge knowing that the more snockered Doc Henry was, the more willing he was to gamble. I also let Doc Henry run up a gambling tab that could be paid off on payday. Sometimes, it got so bad that Doc Henry's entire paycheck was just signed over to the money lenders, and I just happened to be the top money lender on base. Lacking sufficient spending money, Doc Henry would be afraid to go home and face his wife, Aurora, who needed to use the weekly funds for groceries and utility bills. So, he stayed away from home an extra day, and when he did make it home, he physically fought with her when she demanded to know where he had been and more importantly, where the money was. An accomplished seamstress, Aurora supplemented Doc Henry's income with the money she earned from sewing for the officers' wives. But she counted on Doc Henry's salary for the basic necessities to run the household. The more Doc Henry drank and gambled, the more he lost, and the more he had to pay to the money lender on payday. It got so bad that while Aurora was trying to maintain on the little money she earned from sewing, she found herself short of grocery funds almost every Saturday.

This was when I began the second stage of my plan to conquer and acquire the fair Aurora. I would appear in the commissary and be at the checkout stand at the same time that Aurora would be there trying to figure out which items to put back on the shelves. I presented myself as a friend of her husband and would drive her home as a "neighborly gesture," claiming that I owed Doc Henry several favors. I increased my "neighborliness" when I started picking up items from the commissary for her—milk and bread one time; cheese, butter, cereal another time; steaks, chops, chicken and ground beef another time. This "neighborliness" grew to include the entire grocery list, utilities that were about to get shut off for nonpayment, getting school clothes out of layaway, hair appointments, pretty dresses, and ultimately, a trip to Reno, complete with payment for the divorce decree, wedding rings, and a new marriage license. Doc Henry lost his ultimate stash of valuables (his wife and son), and he never even realized that he was gambling with a marked deck of cards!

CHAPTER 9

Aurora

THE CREEK DURING A DROUGHT is a dismal thing. There is some moisture, yes, but there is not enough of it to sustain the comforts of life that existed before the drought. There is just enough moisture to keep the bottom muddy but not enough to foster teeming and rewarding life. The fish in this creek are starving and slowly withering—just like the plant life. The essence of the creek, however, is satisfied. It has done what it was supposed to do—provide moisture to the living things that were strong enough to survive. The quality and quantity of the moisture is not important—just the fact that some life sustaining moisture has been provided.

"Just slap yo momma in the face, Junior. We didn't ask for no baby! Slap yo momma—we don't ask for no baby!" he repeated with an enveloping grin on his face.

"Slap you, Mommy." Junior giggled as he raised his hand to hit me in my face.

"Duarté, stop telling him to act like that. Junior, sit down!"

Junior's twenty-one-month-old frame was standing in the middle of the front seat of the Oldsmobile, wedged in between his daddy, who was driving while chain smoking and complaining, and me holding the newborn Cleodine in my lap with my right hand and attempting to brace Cleophus Jr. with my left hand. *He* had been so loving and caring when we started out. *He* was the one who would rescue me when I was without enough money to pay for gro-

44

ceries at the commissary. *He* was the one who would get my oldest son's school clothes out of layaway when my first husband was off drinking, gambling, and losing his weekly pay. *He* was the one who convinced me to leave that first abusive husband, divorce, and then marry him. *He* promised to take care of me and my child—we would never want for anything.

I had seen the first strains of his anger last year. Henry, my oldest son, was playing choo-choo train with his baby brother, Cleophus Jr. He had the child in a stroller, and they were chugging through the mountains and valleys of the backyard when they ran over a rock. The stroller flipper over and the make-believe engineer fell out onto the ground. His screams brought the engine safety patrol (me) running to see what was wrong. The youngest child survived the fall, but he skinned up his temple, knees, and forearms. The sight of these wounds caused *him* to go into a rage when he came through the front door. *He* had slapped me, his loving wife, hard across the face for allowing "that man's son to inflict harm upon his son." Then he whooped the daylights out of Henry for being so careless. Frightened beyond reason for being only eight years of age, Henry had called his own daddy who lived in San Francisco, crying, and begged him to come and get him. This was all the excuse that Doc Henry needed to put his foot in the oral orifice of the man who had once been his friend but had spirited away his wife who had also been his high school sweetheart. Doc Henry drove the distance from San Francisco to Vallejo with one thought in mind—kicking Cleophus Duarté square in his backsides! He didn't even knock on the door and wait to be invited in. He came through the front and immediately connected his right fist to that thieving man's jaw, knocking him and the chair he was sitting in over. The Pall Mall cigarette that was being sucked upon flew out of Cleophus's mouth and onto the hardwood floor, eventually leaving a permanent burned mark. I grabbed my two sons and ran out of the house to the neighbor's house. I knew that *he* kept a loaded Glock 19 and two cartons of 9 mm bullets in the bedroom locked in his trunk, and I wanted to shield the boys from what could turn into a deadly situation. Those two Air Force men were still thrashing on the floor when the neighborhood husbands came in and pulled them apart. Unobserved by anyone else, Stuart just stood there quietly and watched without saying a word.

"Don't you ever put your hands on my son again, or I'll kill you dead!"

"Can't no child stay in the house with me that I cannot discipline! Take his little ass back with you. He can't stay here no more! And if you ever come around my wife again, I will have your dead body shipped back to yo momma in a cheap worm-eaten wooden box!"

Doc Henry went into the boys' bedroom and stuffed his son's clothing and toys into grocery bags, then he and our son left without saying goodbye.

Life never did return to normal for me. I missed raising both of my sons together. *He* was in his own self house, with his own self family. *He* seemed to be quite happy, making sure that whatever was needed at home (other than love and comfort) was provided. Just like the essence of a creek in a drought.

CHAPTER 10

Aurora

THEY SAY THAT WHEN THE sun shines while it is raining, it means that the devil is beating his wife. The raindrops are her tears of sadness and desolation.

We were living in California, and true to his word, he had provided for our family quite well. He had a knack for earning and saving money. Colored men were rarely allowed to get credit for anything other than overpriced items, and the interest rates on the loans that they qualified for were always a few percentage points higher than that of their white counterparts. For this reason, my husband, Cleophus Duarté, saved his money and paid cash for everything. He always claimed that installment buying was the white man's trick to re-enslave the colored man.

"The items available for the installment plans were of poor quality and overpriced. By the time a colored man has put down a down payment and made three or four of the installments, the white man has already made his money for the value of the item. The rest of it was just gravy on the potatoes! Miss a payment, and the white man will repossess the item and sell it all over again to some other dumb spook who will be happy to get credit from a white man."

We lived in a government housing community while he was saving up for our first real home. He gave me strict instructions on how much money I could spend on groceries and the utility bills. He would soundly smack me in the face if the grocery receipts added up to more than his instructions, if I had to throw out any spoiled food, if the light bill was higher than normal, if I talked on the telephone too long, or if I opened his mail.

He had an automobile, a brand-new Chrysler, that he had paid cash for, but he did not allow me to drive it. He bought for us a modest home in a working-class neighborhood that had a living room, eat-in kitchen, bathroom, and two bedrooms. The banks would not approve him for a regular mortgage loan to purchase a home in a white neighborhood. He refused the terms on the contract that banks would issue to the colored home buyers because the terms were outrageous, according to him. His daddy, Scripture Duarté, had taught him that in order for a man to be a man, he had to have his own self property and at least a thousand dollars' cash available at all times. He paid cash for the home, and he had bank accounts all across the country in his name only. He taught Junior that a man needed to have a million dollars in the bank if he was to consider himself to be a man. I had no idea of how much money he had or even all the banking locations. Our furnishings were purchased from a secondhand furniture store in a wealthy white area of San Rafael because he refused to pay the outrageous prices for brand-new items available for purchase to the colored that were not worth the cost.

As a professional seamstress, I recovered the sofa and chairs in the living room, and I also recovered the chrome dining room chairs with a strong vinyl fabric. I had learned the art of sewing from my mother in Virginia. Sewing, baking, canning, and gardening were skills that all my mother's daughters were taught, plus I had majored in home economics while I was in college, preparing to be a high school teacher. I was the one who exemplified all the lessons taught by both Mom and the Teachers College. He closely watched me on the day that I was making the covers for the dining room chairs. He seemed to be amazed at the dexterity of my fingers as I carefully cut the fabric and applied talcum powder to the vinyl prior to putting it on the sewing machine for the stitching.

"Why are you putting that powder on it?" he had asked.

"To make it soft and pliable. That way, I only have to sew it once. Unlike cloth fabric that you can sew, rip apart, and sew again, vinyl is unforgivable. You can only put needle holes in it once. Once the needle has pierced vinyl, that needle hole stays forever, and you cannot repair it. You either have a flawed item or you have to discard it and start all over again with a fresh piece."

He had snorted. "That is kind of like a marriage. Stuart tells me that when you put a hole in it, that hole is always there. If you stay in it, you have a flawed relationship, or you can discard it and start all over again with someone fresh. What do you think about that? Hah!"

The house on Lemon Street had a large front yard and side yard along with a sizable backyard. I wanted to plant fruit trees and a vegetable garden in the back, but he thwarted my plans by pouring a concrete patio that took up the entire area with the exception of an eighteen-inch border along the fence line. Not giving up my dream, I planted along that border just as my mother planted along the sides of the house at home in Virginia—a vegetable and then a flower. Mom had always said, "Flowers are real nice, but if you only have just one square foot of dirt to plant in, you need to plant you something you can eat first. Then if there is room, you can put in a pretty flower."

I had sweet potatoes, tomatoes, bush beans, onions, and strawberry plants interspersed with carnations, lilies, nasturtium, and azaleas. The front and side yards were reserved for my pride and joy—roses! I had beds of red roses, white roses, pink roses, and yellow roses. There were tea roses, Grandiflora roses, carpet roses, and miniature roses. They were along the inside of the white picket fence that framed the property and in a bed under the large evergreen tree in the front yard. Passersby would stop to admire those roses and speak kindly to the lady who was watering them. No matter how hot it was, *he* forbade me to wear shorts while working in the yard because, according to him, it was unnecessary advertising. *He* also forbade me to do any of the laborious tasks associated with maintaining a beautiful yard during the populated hours when someone might see that I was doing it and not *he*. I could only cut the grass, cultivate the soil, prune, weed, or apply steer manure before 7:00 a.m. or after the sun had gone down.

He had a strict rule regarding the mail. No one was to open his own self mail! There was a chest freezer on sale at Montgomery Wards that I had my eyes on, and *he* had told me that there was no money available for it. Wow, if I only had a way to freeze my fresh vegetables and fruits, I wouldn't have to go through the labor of canning and storing. When the letter from the IRS came addressed to Mr. and Mrs. Cleophus Duarté, I felt that it would be okay to open it, so I did. It was an income tax refund check, and it was in an amount that could cover the cost of the chest freezer with some leftover. I was ecstatic and could not wait for him to come home so that I could share the news with him. *He* always came in from his job at Travis Air Force Base, went first to the bathroom, and then settled down in his chair to smoke, read the mail and the *Wall Street Journal.* I always placed the mail on the small table next to his chair so that it would be available for him as soon as he sat down. *He* had sat down and was preparing to light one of his filter less Pall Mall cigarettes when *he* froze and stared at the stack of mail.

"Aurora! Who in the hell opened my mail?" he screamed.

"But, Duarté, it was addressed to Mr. and Mrs. I am the Mrs. Doesn't that give me the right to open mail that is addressed to me as well as you?"

"Woman, what did I tell you? I told you to *never* open my mail. That mail is my own self business and none of yours. I told you that I would kill you if you ever opened my mail! The only reason that you are alive today is because Stuart told me to let you live!"

He then slapped me wickedly across the face, causing my lip to bleed.

"Duarté, please! I am sorry!"

When *he* slammed me against the wall and moved toward the bedroom, I was thankful that I had previously removed the bullets from the Glock revolver that *he* kept locked in his chest and buried them in the backyard under a tomato bush. True to my suspicions, *he* went directly to the trunk, opened it, and pulled out his Glock. *He* pointed it at my head and pulled the trigger! *He* seemed perplexed that it did not go off and started cussing to himself. This short interval gave me time to run out of the house and across the street to the

Palmer family's home even though I was not fully clothed. Because of the heat, I had been doing my housework clothed only in my undergarments and a full slip. This was not the first time that I had sought shelter from a caring neighbor when *he* was on a frenzy of destruction with my physical annihilation as his ultimate goal. Mother Beatrice could always pray him back to a sensible reality when *he* got like this, and I was counting on her this time.

I collapsed in Mother Beatrice's arms, and I cried and cried and cried. I cried because my husband was pathologically abusive. I cried because I was in California virtually alone. My entire family resided on the East Coast. I cried because I had lost my eldest son due to his maniacal jealousy and need to be in control—not to mention his evilness. I cried because his physical treatment of me hurt, and his psychological treatment of me hurt even more. I cried because I had not listened to my mother, who had implored me to not divorce Doc Henry.

"When God made man, he put a cup of dog meat in each one's recipe. Some of them got more issued to 'em than others, but they all have at least a cupful. When you chose that man, you chose him and everything he is made up of. You stood up in church before God and said that you would love and honor that man until death do you part, and now you're planning to leave him for another man! You don't leave your husband because his breath stank. The next one will harbor stank in his feet, his head or some other area. Shucks, girl! Something stanks on all of them! You need to put this in the hands of the Lord and pray."

Pray I did. I prayed that Duarté would not kill me one day. It seemed that my only purpose was to provide him with a son of his own. *He* didn't need me anymore. I continued to cry because I had given up a relationship with a man I had grown up with and who still needed to grow up only to assume a relationship with a man who needed to be in a mental institution. I cried because I was afraid. I was married to the devil. My tears fell like big raindrops. The raindrops were my tears of sadness and desolation.

Chapter 11

Aurora

The state of California was building a new highway that would come from Benicia into Vallejo. It was to be called Highway 780, and it was scheduled to enter right where our house stood on Lemon Street. The family had to move. He was already in Spokane, so I had to manage the move by myself. He didn't seem too anxious for the family to come to Spokane. He had purchased some rental property less than a mile from the Lemon Street residence, and he instructed me to tell the tenants they had to move because the children and I were moving in. When I talked with the renters, they showed me a paid-up lease that gave the family another six months of residence, and they were not going to move until then. So I called Duarté and told him that the two kids and I were coming—period!

We caught the train up to Spokane, Washington, and the children were as excited as I was dreading the reunion with my husband. The only incident that caused concern on the train was when I had my dentures soaking in a glass set on the side of the sink in their compartment. Cleodine needed to use the toilet, so she raised up the sink to expose the toilet bowl. In doing so, everything on the sink that was not bolted down was immediately disposed of. I watched this in slow motion and in horror, and I tried to stop the sink from closing totally. I was only able to save my bottom dentures. I must have screamed!

"Cleodine, what are you doing? You just threw away my teeth! My teeth!"

The conductor heard the commotion and quickly came to see if he could be of assistance. He could not. All he could do was try to calm me down and comfort my little girl who was so ashamed that she had made her mommy angry. Both of us were in tears. Me because I did not want my husband to see me without my top dentures, and little Cleodine because she had caused her mommy to cry.

I had sent to him the particulars of our travel arrangements, so I was morbidly puzzled when he did not meet us at the train station. He was always claiming that he had someone watching me. Had that someone seen me without my upper dentures? Nonsense! I tried to call him at work, and he was not there. I tried to call him at home, and there was no answer. Maybe he was on his way. I waited for two hours and then called the Air Force base requesting to speak with his commanding officer. Two and a half hours later, an officer from the base appeared, holding high over his head a sign with the name Duarté on it. I waved him toward where I was sitting, and the children were sleeping. He informed me that he had been sent to pick the family up and get them settled in a hotel room until my husband could meet us. He was in the hospital suffering with pneumonia. I accepted the officer's graciousness. The officer checked me and the children into a hotel room with one large bed. All three of us slept there for the next two days, taking our meals in the diner downstairs.

When he was discharged from the hospital, he came to get us, and he took us to the house he had procured. It was a single-story home with kitchen, living room, bathroom, two bedrooms, mudroom, and a basement for laundry and playing. That first night in Spokane, he slapped me repeatedly for coming when he had told me not to. He slapped me for not coming to the hospital to see about him.

"You just laid up in that hotel on your fat tail and didn't even think about me lying up in that hospital. I could have died!"

I tearfully tried to explain to him that the family renting the house had a legal right to stay there for six more months. He had taken a year's worth of rent in advance, and their lease was not up yet. I could not legally force them to move. As for not coming to the hospital, Junior was seven and Cleodine was five. They were too young to come into the hospital, and I didn't know anyone who could keep them while I was gone. The explanations meant nothing to him. The next day, I was seen in the commissary, shopping for groceries and other household necessities. The facial bruises and swollen lip were quite evident, but not one person made a comment to me about it. It was none of their business.

Chapter 12

Aurora

As soon as the lease on that rental property was up, the children and I moved back to Vallejo. I filed for divorce. He begged me not to go through with it. He claimed that he was sick, and he was getting medical help. He just needed me to be patient with him. The knowledge that I was three months pregnant with his third child was a contributing factor in my decision to stay in the marriage.

The rental house that he had bought previously was in a diverse neighborhood that contained several immigrant families. They seemed to be impervious to the belief that colored neighbors would bring down the value of their property. Perhaps they had not been in the United States long enough to become engorged with the racism that exists here. In any event, we all got along quite well. Germans lived next door across the alley, and from them the children learned about the real Santa Claus and how to eat strudel. The Italians lived four blocks up the street, moving to their school, unable to speak English. The Italian children learned the playground vernacular and, within a year, the classroom verbiage. Cleodine was amazed to learn that spaghetti sauce took all day to cook as opposed to simply being poured out of a jar. The Filipinos also lived in the neighborhood. Their dad amazed the children in the neighborhood with his pleasure of eating pickled fish eyeballs while his wife served *lumpia* to the girls who came to visit and play with their daughters. The Puerto Ricans lived at the end of the alley where there was always something lively

going on: calypso music, laughter, dancing, and outdoor grilling—
Puerto Rican style. The Korean family lived midway down the left
side of the alley. The mother enjoying morning coffee and chatter
with me whenever *he* was not around. When *he* was home, this Asian
neighbor could not come into the house. *He* told me that Stuart had
convinced him that Mrs. Do and her family were all spies sent to see
what he was doing.

The Korean neighbor had once inquired if *he* was a writer. She
always heard that Underwood typewriter clacking away whenever
she was passing down the alley. I considered the inquiry as a com-
pliment and relayed it to *him*. *He* kept an even more watchful eye
on that Korean family from that day on. The Korean wife could not
come into his residence for coffee, and her son could not come onto
the property to play either.

There was a family of white people named Hitchcock who lived
midway down the alley on the right side. *He* ruthlessly referred to
them as poor white trash who would kill a colored man as quickly
as they could spit out the word *nigger*. Our daughter, Cleodine,
believed this because the first time she was called the "N" word,
it was by one of these children. One of the girl twins, Carrie, had
admonished Cleodine at recess one day after she had been chastised
in class for not being able to successfully spell a word. Cleodine had
quickly raised her hand and offered the correct spelling. Carrie had
confronted Cleodine during recess by the monkey bars. "You think
you are so smart, but you are nothin' but a little ole nigger gal." And
she had sauntered off in an Elvis Presley–mannered stride. When
Cleodine recounted the incident to us that night during dinner, *his*
coal-black complexion turned ashy gray, and he just sat there in a
catatonic state until tears clouded his eyes and began to drop onto
his dinner plate. He got up from the table and left the home, walking, not returning until three hours later. By the time he returned,
the children had been bathed and put to bed. Their school clothes
were laid out for the next day. Their lunchboxes were packed with a
sandwich, two apricots, carrot sticks, milk, and a Twinkie. The food
had been put away, dishes washed, garbage taken out, and the floor
swept and mopped. With him taking on that deathly countenance, I

didn't want anything to go wrong, to tilt him over the brink of that chasm between anger and rage because I would ultimately be the target of his wrath.

When he came back, he smoked a complete pack of Pall Mall cigarettes before he spoke to me. He talked to me about Newton, Mississippi, and his memories of the N-word. He recounted stories of whiskered white men dragging him by his head in their automobile, of black men flogged, sometimes to death, of lynchings, rapes, and legal confiscation of property because the whites felt the word *nigger* separated real people from beings no better than animals. If a Negro hit a white man, he could be shot or lynched. A white man who killed a Negro received no comeuppance. He was just doing what he was supposed to do. He told me about how hard it was to be a man with coal-black skin not only in Mississippi, but in the armed forces as well. He wanted his children to grow up and be educated in California, so they would never have to live life as a nigger. And a trashy white neighbor child had invaded his sanctuary. He had put the call in to his best friend, Stuart, and they had spent these three hours just walking, talking, and thinking. Their thoughts ranged from doing nothing, which was Mississippi Negro style to going on a militaristic mission and eradicating the imposed threat of the entire white family that lived midway down the alley on the right side. He and Stuart had gone over the potential remedies:

1) He could burn their house down at night with the entire family in it.

2) He could lie in wait in the bushes in the alley near their home and take them out one by one with the German pistol he kept locked in his trunk.

3) He could poison some apples for their bastard kids and liquor for the trash-ass parents and leave it all in a box on their front porch. They would all be demised within twenty-four hours.

4) He could mix finely ground glass into a two-pound bag of granulated white sugar and substitute it for the bag that the county welfare left on their porch each month.

They came up with several ways that he could eradicate them, thus saving his family from the wrath of their upcoming treachery. He told me that he and Stuart had agreed that he should talk it over with me, his wife, and sleep on it before deciding.

I convinced him to let me talk to the principal of the school the children attended.

"He ain't gonna do nuthin', I tell you. But I will give you twenty-four hours to try it your way. Then I am going on a reconnaissance mission to solve the problem myself!"

I reported to the principal the next morning, and he quickly brought Cleodine and several other children witnesses to testify to what they had seen and heard. Convinced that they were telling the truth, he contacted the perpetrator's parents and informed them about the actions of their eldest daughter and the consequence he was going to apply—the principal's board of education. The board was a flat panel about twenty inches in length and five inches in width, half inch in depth with nickel-sized holes randomly drilled in to intensify the effect. Carrie got ten whacks on her buttocks. When *he* heard of the punishment, *he* was satisfied that no further intervention on his part was required. *He* also resolved to continue with his plan to have his children live and be educated only in the Golden State of California. After conferring with Stuart, they mutually agreed to totally abandon his plans to punish that white family. They would present no more problems. He did, however, add the Hitchcock family to the list of people who were not allowed to come onto his property for any reason.

Chapter 13

Cleodine

Physical discipline can be the catalyst to spark the understanding of rules—not the *why* but the *what*. What will happen as a consequence of breaking the rule … if caught?

I could always tell when *he* was home. I could hear the *clack, clack, clack* of the old Underwood typewriter. By the way, no one ever saw anything that *he* had written. *He* kept his papers locked up in his trunk, so people could not "see what he was doing." I could smell the smoke from his filterless Pall Mall cigarettes that he chain-smoked daily, and I could not hear the sounds of the afternoon stories "Search for Tomorrow," "As the World Turns," the "Secret Storm," and "General Hospital" that generally greeted me when I came in from school. Mommy usually had these stories on while she cooked, washed, sewed and ironed—that is when *he* was not there. When *he* was there, the television could only be on for the five o'clock news, the *Ed Sullivan Show*, and the late-night show. Since we children had to go to bed by 7:00 p.m. each night, this meant only the news for us during the week. No amount of crying and pleading could convince *him* to let us stay up past 7:00 p.m. to watch Walt Disney or any other show that aired from 7:00 p.m. on. Nor could we watch cartoons like *Heckle and Jeckle* or sitcoms like *The Little Rascals* or the *Amos and Andy Show*. He declared that the producers of these shows conspired to depict colored people in a negative light.

Music was frivolous in his mind. His children were going to develop their brains—not practice singing and dancing for a living. No wonder he discontinued Cleophus Jr.'s accordion lessons when he was seven and made Mommy get back the down payment she had made on Sister Thompson's upright piano that she had procured for my upcoming piano lessons the year that I turned five.

Ugh! I had seen Mommy measuring out those despicable dried lima beans last night for a long soak and a slow simmer with a piece of salt pork for flavoring. Ugh! No amount of seasoning was going to make those pasty and tasteless things palatable, and they were going to be served for dinner tonight! Ugh! Each legume was about the size of a quarter. Too big to swallow down whole, I had to bite into each one, unleashing that nasty mush into my eight-year old mouth. Ugh! In *his* house, you did not dare say that you didn't like something. You ate what was on your plate or you faced the application of *his* whipping strap.

Now some kids prepared for a butt whipping by stuffing their clothes with wadded-up paper that, if not discovered, could absorb the blows. I knew that I was not going to eat that vegetable that I imagined tasted like parakeet droppings, and I also knew that my refusal meant that a butt whipping was on the horizon of that evening, so I devised a scheme. First, I had the whipping strap hidden under a bundle of his newspapers. Then I folded up a piece of wax paper into the top of my sock. Dinner was served. We had those dreadful lima beans, white rice, meatloaf, and cornbread. While *he* playfully haggled with Junior over who would get to eat the salt pork, I sneakily placed my lima beans one by one into that wax paper holding well in my sock. I had stashed about half of my ration of lima beans safely away from my mouth when I asked to be excused to go to the restroom. The plan was to dump those nasty beans into the toilet, flush them down, and then return for the remainder and a repeat performance. As I passed by Junior, he noticed my bulging sock and exclaimed, "What's wrong with your foot? It's all swelled up!"

Caught! *He* examined my foot himself, recognized the stash of dinner proteins, and made me take them out of their sock haven, put them back on my plate, and then *he* force-fed them to me. When I gagged, *he* just spooned up the carnage and refed it to me. My sweet Lord Jesus! I was miserable, nauseous, frightened, and developing stronger dislike for my father by the minute. The final piece of the punishment for breaking the on your plate rule was to be the butt whipping. *He* searched for his whipping strap and could not find it, so *he* just turned me over his knee and began to spank my backsides with the palm of his hand. I had not anticipated this, and I lost everything in me through every sphincter-like opening in my young body. Tears flowed from my eyes, and mucous flowed from my nose. Lima beans regurgitated from my throat. Urine dribbled from my bladder, and liquid feces oozed from my anus. It all landed on *him*! Disgusted and outdone, *he* let me up and yelled for Mommy to "clean that child's mess up!"

He himself went out into the backyard to hose himself off. The evidence was all over his pants, shirt, and shoes. *He* left the wet clothes on the back porch for Mommy to clean, went into the bathroom to bathe himself clean, put on fresh pajamas and spent the rest of the evening smoking those filterless Pall Mall cigarettes and clacking away on that Underwood typewriter. That night, *he* didn't even bother to put any typing paper in it.

From that point on, we were not allowed to go to the bathroom during mealtime. *He* would routinely bring a freshly cut switch to the dinner table to capture the attention of a "think you are smarter than me" child who didn't want to obey his "what's on your plate" rule.

Junior and I worked out several schemes between us to solve the problem and indeed "outsmart" the mean daddy. Rather than ask to go to the bathroom, we would simply pass objectionable food to each other under the table—right under his nose. Junior did not like greens or mashed potatoes while I did not like lima beans or liver, so we each relieved the other of the offensive items of cuisine. We didn't really understand the *why* of the "what's on your plate" rule, but we each thoroughly understood the *what*. We cooperatively worked out a resolution that would meet two objectives: the non-consumption of despised food items and the avoidance of a butt whipping for breaking the "what's on your plate" rule.

CHAPTER 14

Cleodine

WHO ARE *THEY?* THE QUESTION permeated us through our youth years as food coloring permeates the water in a vase of white flowers eventually changing their color. It transformed. He used to admonish us daily with "Get your education. It is something that they cannot ever take away from you."

My six-year-old mind chockfull with visions of monsters and boogeymen could picture the *they* as invisible beings from Mars that would snatch up an unwary kid's schoolwork. I had no explanation of what *they* would do with some kid's schoolwork.

My twelve-year-old mind could not conjure who the *they* were or why *they* would want to even attempt to take someone else's grades away. At that impressionable age, I saw grades as a way of parents controlling a kid's behavior. If you get bad grades, you get a whooping in my father's house. If you get good grades, well, that is what you are supposed to do. So how could taking away the grades of someone who was not even in your family be of any value to you?

The high school mind began to realize that knowledge was paired with economic success. The educated Negroes in town lived in the nicer homes that had more than one bathroom, a den, and a formal dining room. These educated Negroes gave the most tithes in church, wore the expensive clothes, went to Disneyland during the summer break, and they drove the biggest luxury cars with air conditioning and leather seats.

History and sociology classes in college taught me that throughout history, people of all ethnicities (especially people of color and women) had been supplanted, victimized, terrorized, and subsidized by the establishment—often losing title to property, freedom, and lives by pseudolegal means. The *they* were the privileged wealthy of all ethnicities who fought to maintain their economic status by any means.

As a retired educator, grandparent, divorcee and widow, I recollect having seen *them* take all kinds of things away from people. Installment loan items, automobiles, personal residences, oil and other natural resources, means of making a living, health benefits, titles, the allegedly biting dog, rotten teeth, ruptured and non-ruptured appendices, children, right to give birth to children, malignant and nonmalignant tumors, the right to vote, the right to live in this country, the right to pursue happiness—almost anything tangible can be taken away. What cannot be taken is the knowledge and educational achievement that you have strived for and obtained. Hence, "Get your education. It is something that they cannot ever take away from you." The meaning is now understood.

CHAPTER 15

Cleodine

WHEN MOMMY ANNOUNCED THAT WE were going to Virginia to visit the grandparents; we kids were excited. We were unaware that Mommy was taking us there for our own safety because *he* had threatened to burn us all up in the house! His house! He was in New York on business, and Stuart had been watching the house and the family for him while he was gone and had reported seeing a male visitor having "coffee" with Mommy one Sunday afternoon after church. Enraged, *he* had called Mommy on the telephone and told her what his plans for her and the children were. *He* was going to come to California and get Junior. The rest of us damned kids and our pet dog would burn up in the house with her!

Mommy had gone up to Travis AFB to talk to someone about her husband. They shuttled her off to three different offices, and in the last office, she was told that she would need to confer with a physician who was stationed in San Rafael. She spent another day gaining access to this latest physician who did finally see her. She was ushered into his office, a stale office painted puke green and filled with military issue furnishings. She sat down in front of him and asked him point-blank, "What is wrong with my husband?" The doctor didn't answer her right away. He just kept leafing through a manila file folder in front of him that had to be at least three inches thick. He would glance over at her over the top of his horn-rimmed glasses after every few pages and then avert his eyes back to his task.

Since he would not talk to her, she started to talk to him. She told of when they met and married, his fight with her oldest son's father, his sole control of the family finances, his mood changes, his preoccupation with dirt and germs, his suspicions, his acts of violence against her including the time he pointed a German pistol at her head and pulled the trigger! Thank God she had rummaged through the trunk, found the gun, and unloaded it. He was forever typing on that black Underwood typewriter, yet she had never seen even one document that he had produced. He had refused to take her to the hospital when I was born. He had just purchased a new Oldsmobile, and he didn't want her messing up his upholstery with that baby that he didn't ask her for. He had just fiddled around for hours with excuses of he couldn't find his keys, then the engine would not start, and then he needed to go and get petroleum for it. He was out getting the petroleum when I was born at home. Mommy had to call the base hospital to send an ambulance for her and me, her newborn infant. He made it home with the gas tank full just in time to take over the care of Junior while his wife and newborn daughter were being driven to the base hospital.

He was unreasonably stern with his children, although there were times when he demonstrated just how powerful a parent he could be. She told of when he would take the tubes out of the television set and tell us children that the set was broken. He would walk us to the public library and let us check out the maximum number of books allowed. Then he would expect book reports on each of the books we had read. He would hold mathematics class every evening in the kitchen after dinner for the two oldest of us utilizing his Air Force textbooks. Junior caught on real fast, but I had a hard time understanding algebraic equations at the tender age of nine. He would whoop me for not understanding.

Mommy went on and on about her mysterious and frightening husband. She completed her story with his latest threat. He claimed that his best friend, Stuart, had been keeping an eye on the family and his property while he was away, and Stuart had reported seeing her having coffee in his house with a male suitor one Sunday afternoon. A man from the church had offered to give us a ride home from church that day. Since he never left his car for her to drive, she had to walk everywhere she went, borrow a neighbor's car, or accept a ride from someone. It was terribly hot that day, and she accepted a ride home for herself and us. She offered to give that kind man a couple of dollars for gasoline, but he had said no. He was about to drive to Stockton to pick up his wife and children from their grandparents' home. He would, however, appreciate a cold drink to take in the car with him. Mommy had gone into the house and come back with a mason jar filled with grape Kool-Aid, lemon slices, and ice cubes—not a cup of coffee. The man had never come into the house, and she did not drink the beverage with him. Stuart must have been going blind!

My father had heard of this encounter and turned it into something that was not. His response was to call her and say that he was coming to get Junior, and then he was going to burn the house up with her, the dog, and the rest of the children in it! Mommy was afraid that he would do just that.

"And that's why I am here. I need help. I need to know what is wrong with my husband so that I can figure out how I can live with him."

The doctor just closed the manila folder, tapped his pencil on the cover five times, and told her succinctly, "I can't tell you what is in this file, but I will tell you that I have seen cases like this before, and it is not unusual for the patient to just snap one day, kill his entire family and himself. You need to get you and your children out of that house as quickly as possible. I will arrange to have him picked up and readmitted to the hospital."

When she left the doctor's office, she went immediately to a telephone booth. Her sister-in-law, Helen, who worked for AT&T, and she could arrange to patch her through to her parents in Virginia at no cost.

"Mom, this is Aurora. I can't talk now, but I need to bring the children to Virginia now."

"You know you can always come home, Aurora. I know you were having a hard time with that man all the way out there in California, but as long as you were willing to stay there and put up with it, I had nothing to say. You can always come home. There will always be room for all of you here. And if that cottonmouth snake dares to come onto me and Dilly's land, he will know something for sure."

"He won't come after us, Mom. The Air Force is going to put him into the hospital."

CHAPTER 16

Cleodine

THE SCHOOL YEAR WAS 1958–1959. School families routinely regulate the calendar according to when the children are in school and when they are out for the summer. That particular school year, I learned so much about life and how racial restrictions can impact what one is allowed to do, feel, and dream to become. It started when we boarded the Greyhound bus in Vallejo, California bound for the country residence of Mommy's parents. They were William Sherman Logan and Ida Elizabeth Logan, and they lived in rural Halifax County, Virginia.

Most of the trip back east was uneventful. Junior and I played on the large back seat of the bus, and Karol Ann, the baby, slept in Mommy's arms. Junior and I played checkers, hangman, war—you name it. We entertained ourselves by going up to the front of the bus whenever the seat behind the driver was empty. We would ply the driver with questions: "Where are we?" "When do we get there?" "What is the name of that bridge?" The driver would smile at us, answer our questions until he directed us to go back to our mother so that he could drive in peace. All the while, smiling. The first part of our education that year occurred when we got past the Mason Dixon line. Mommy would not let us go to the front of the bus to bug the driver anymore. We thought that perhaps this particular driver just didn't like kids, so we stayed on our back seat and played games.

At one of the bus stops, some white children about our ages boarded the bus. Together, we kids all had a grand time on that back seat, playing the games, laughing, and talking about our schools and pets back at home. Like me and Junior, the white children wanted to go up to the empty seat behind the driver and query him with the typical questions that children ask. Only, Mommy would not let us go. Her answer to our "Why not?" was "Because I said so." Junior and I watched as our new friends slid into the seat behind the driver and questioned him. This particular driver seemed to be the friendliest of them all. He gave the children some hard candy, which they shared with us when they returned to the back seat.

At the next bus stop, everybody had to get off the bus for an hour. As children, we knew what the first stop had to be—the restroom. We all headed for the restroom section. To our surprise, there were signs posted on the walls—Colored and White. The white children went straight into the white restroom section while Junior and I headed for the colored restroom section since the other colored passengers were going there. Our combined curiosities and imaginations were inflamed. We had never before been in a bathroom with the fixtures in any color other than white. I was hoping that the girls' side would be pink, and I figured that the boys' side would be either blue or green. Much to our dismay, the fixtures were typical white porcelain! Humph! False advertising! The next puzzlement came at the water fountains. We saw the Colored and White signs again. Maybe the water in the colored fountain was in a rainbow burst of color! What! It was just plain water! We spotted our white friends at a lunch counter eating ice cream and wanted to join them. We found Mommy and asked for some money for the ice cream. She said, "No." The look on her face let us know that we were not to ask the traditional "Why?" The answer was "No," and that was the end of it.

As we neared our destination, I became increasingly aware that the white passengers always took seats at the front of the bus. There was a short piece of wood on the floor about two-thirds of the way down, and the passengers who looked like the Duarté family started taking their seats there and filling up all the way to the back. Junior and I no longer had the large back seat to ourselves. Other adult passengers who looked like us also sat there. We couldn't understand why an adult would want to sit on a back seat with a couple of squirming kids when there were plenty of seats up at the front of the bus.

School was starting soon, and Junior and I were going to attend the country school in Halifax. Mommy bought us new shoes in downtown Halifax, ordered new clothing for Cleophus out of the Sears catalogue, and she made me a dozen new school dresses. Grandma would pack our lunch each day in lard buckets. We usually had a chicken or meatloaf sandwich, an apple turnover, some nuts and fruit (some grapes, a peach, or a pear). The typical fare for the other children was a peanut butter or bacon sandwich (not even wrapped in wax paper—just stuck in a bag) and a wrinkled old apple. We walked about a quarter of a mile down a red clay road to the bus stop. While we waited for our bus, a modern school bus with white school children would pass us by. Eventually, the bus for the colored children would rattle up and stop to let the passengers on. I rationalized that the first bus was already full, and that was why we had to wait for the second bus. That bus relegated for the colored children appeared rattling and shaking. There was glass missing from some of the windows. In the hot months, screens were taped over these openings to keep the bugs out. In the cold months, large sheets of plastic were taped over these openings to keep the snow out.

The colored school bus passed the white school, a red-brick building with manicured lawns, swings, tetherball poles, basketball hoops, baseball diamonds, a track field—all the things that our school in California had. The school for the colored children was a wooden three-room structure with two rows of outhouses in the back. One classroom housed kindergarten and first and second grades. Another classroom housed third, fourth, and fifth grades. The third classroom housed sixth, seventh, and eighth grades. Thus, for the first time ever, Junior and I were in the same classroom! The restroom outhouses were horrible! There were flies and ants everywhere! Frequently, a wasp nest could be menacingly seen up in one of the corners. Each side was designated for either girls or boys and consisted of an open bench with six toilet holes carved out over a trench. Lime was in the trench, but it did not stifle the smell. The indignity of not having stalls for privacy was just too much. To add to that, there was a water pump and a large sink for handwashing, and the only soap was a piece of lye soap that everyone shared and no paper towels. Children just either shook their hands dry or dried them on their clothes—if they washed their hands at all. It was at this juncture in my life that I learned to "hold it" all day long and wait until I got back home to the sanitation of my grandparents' home to relieve myself.

The school officials wanted to put me and Junior each two grades over where we should have been, but Mommy had said, "No." We would just be put back in the right grades when we got back home in California. So I entered the third grade, and Junior entered the fifth grade. So many of the children could not read well or do math well. It was amazing. The teacher used us, the new kids from California, to help the other students who needed extra attention. Helpers we were. Smart we were. But when the teacher decided that the class was being too noisy, she whipped the backs of every child in the classroom—including the two from California who could read, write, and do math so well. Back at home, the principal only paddled students who got into fights, used foul language, or talked back to their teachers. I had never heard of a teacher beating the backs of every child in a classroom with a large switch just because they "chatted" too much. After she beat us all, she dared us to keep crying with the threat, "Quiet down, or I'll give you something else to cry about!" We needed no more admonition.

Recess time was a frightening experience. Nasty boys would always try to look into the girls' outhouse, so a team of girls would routinely block the entrance while their friends, sisters, or cousins were inside relieving themselves. Girls who did not have a bevy of friends, sisters, or cousins to protect them would suffer at the hands of these nasty boys. Those nasty boys would peek on girls while they were in the restroom, and they would "feel" on them while they were at recess. The practice of "feeling" on a girl was perpetrated daily. If the nasty boy did not run up to a girl and pat his hand on her vaginal area and then run away, he would cup her derriere when she passed by or was standing in line at the water pump. Of course, if the girl told on the boy, he would get a sound beating from the teacher. Consequently, his girl family members would pound the tattler to a pulp after school. If there were significant members of each family enrolled in the same school, a feud the likings of a black Hatfield and McCoy would start and might last for weeks. To avoid all that, most of the girls would just bear the sexual assault and say nothing.

The colored school did not have the type of playground equipment that the white school had and that Junior and I were accustomed to. Parents fashioned kick balls out of pieces of old rubber tires tied together with twine. Softballs were made the same way, and the bats were thick branches cut to the appropriate size. Jump ropes were long dogwood tree switches that were debarked and braided into ropes. The favorite game to play was "pop the whip." The longer the line of children, the more forceful the whip could pop. Only the bravest or least suspecting child would dare be the last child on a "pop the whip" chain.

Now, Willie Mills was one of those nasty boys who used to sneak up on girls and sexually assault them. He had felt on me twice already, and I told each time. His girl relatives did not beat me up because I had a bevy of girl relatives at that school myself, and they would have pounded his girls to a pulp. Willie Mills would feel up on a girl, would take his whooping from the teacher, and then run outside and raucously laugh about it. Within weeks, he would violate some girl again—one who might be afraid to tell. One day while I was at the water pump, I saw Willie Mills heading in my direction. I got out of line and ran to catch up with my cousins Kathy and Doris. Kathy could punch as hard as a boy could, so I knew I would be safe in her presence. I saw Willie scowling, and he pointed at me and yelled out, "I'll get cha. Wait until lunchtime, you stinkin' skunk!" I had two hours to figure out a way to keep Willie Mills away from me at lunchtime. I carefully devised a plan. There would be a monster "pop the whip" line at lunchtime, and Willie would be the last person on the line! He would be flipped on his big black butt, and everyone would laugh at him. I started a rumor amongst the third graders that the line was going to be a monster and that Willie Mills was afraid to be on the end. He was nothing but a big black chicken!

This challenge moved slowly at first, but by the time it reached the fifth-grade rows in the classroom, it was alive and fed as well as a suckling pig lying on its side, waiting in anticipation for the next stage of feeding. Somehow, it also moved over into the sixth, seventh, and eighth grade side of the school. There was no way for Willie to back down now.

Normally, when there was going to be a "pop the whip" line during lunch, everybody ate their lunch first and then descended onto the grass area to play. On this particular day, lunches were stored outside under the trees so that everyone who wanted to either participate or spectate could do so. The largest children routinely lined up first, smaller children in the middle, and the strongest children on the end. With a small "pop the whip" game, ten to fifteen children would line up, grasp hands, and play. The line would start its movement by the first child, and when the right momentum had been reached, that first child would stop, and one by one, the other children would stop with the last child being "popped." To be "popped" usually meant that the last child was flipped and rolled over in the grass. If he was strong enough, he could withstand the centrifugal force and maintain his stance. If he was not strong enough, he routinely landed on his butt and rolled over a few times amid the laughter of the other children. Because of the challenge made to one of the nastiest boys in the school, Willie Mills, the line this day was unusually long.

There must have been sixty-five to seventy children in the line with Willie Mills at the end. Big Black Betty, an eighth grader, was the first person in the line. She instructed each child to grasp the children on either side not by the hands, but by the wrists. This would make a stronger whip and lessen the chance of someone getting hurt. Nasty Willie Mills waited until everyone was in place, and then he strutted over to the end of the line. When he passed by me, he grabbed his crotch and shook it at me. This action brought about some laughter, some in admiration, and some in nervousness. Big Black Betty counted to ten, and she started the line to move. It was customary for the line to make one complete circle before "popping," but Big Black Betty moved that line three times before she stopped the momentum. It seemed like it took forever for the line to "pop," and when it did, at least six children were flipped over onto the grass. Boy, it was great! There was laughter as the children who were flipped got up with grass stains all over their clothes. Some shirts were torn, hair was tangled with grass, dirt, and what looked like mud. As quickly as the laughter started, it ebbed, slowed down, and then there was silence. Everyone was waiting for Willie Mills to get up and take his comeuppance because he was one of the ones not strong enough to withstand the "pop" in spite of his boastfulness. "Get up, Willie." Willie Mills still did not move. Most of the children crowded around him while some of the others ran for the teachers.

"Pop the whip" games were banned in the Halifax County schools from that day on. Willie Mills died that day from a broken neck sustained when he flipped over more voraciously than even he could have imagined. He would never "feel" on girls again. He would never run out of the school laughing after receiving a beating from the teacher for his violations. He would never answer the challenge of being a big black chicken again, and he would never grow up into whoever he could have been.

I hated Willie Mills because of the way that he humiliated and sexually assaulted me, and I planned for an activity that would have him falling on his butt and being humiliated in front of the entire school. He was an evil nasty boy, but did he deserve to die for his nastiness? Did I have the right to plan his execution? What if we never had come to Virginia? Something like this would never have happened in California! In the first place, where Junior and I lived in California, colored and white children went to school together. Our school principal, Mr. Raciot (pronounced Rosco) would not have allowed a boy to sexually intimidate a girl. My cousins would not have had to take action against the perpetrator. Mr. Raciot would have had him removed from the school. Teachers would not have beaten children with switches. The average colored child would not be two to three grades behind his white counterparts. All the schools would have had decent and clean lavatories with stall walls, soap, and paper towels—not an open trench filled with lime. There would not have been ants, flies, and wasps in the lavatory. There would have had decent playground equipment and decent accommodations in the school. Children would have clean clothes to wear to school every day, and not the same outfit each day for a week before getting laundered. We would have fresh milk delivered to the classrooms on a daily basis, and good food for lunch. We would have adequate textbooks—not used textbooks from the white school that colored parents had to either purchase or encourage the children to learn without benefit of a textbook.

For years, I felt that I was somehow responsible for Nasty Willie Mills's death. In time, I came to the realization of what segregation does to a child on an intimate basis. When you grow up having to accept the fact that you are less than someone else because of the color of your skin, you can grow into a self-hater. The stark contrast of the white school building with all its playgrounds and supplies and the colored school building with its outhouses sets the stage the moment the child ventures from the safety of home to the beginning of an education or miseducation. The children called the darkest of the children black. The blacker the child was, the more he or she was despised by personal ethnic counterparts. Sometimes this despising was because the perpetrator actually felt superior to this darker image of himself, or it could be because the perpetrator recognized the advantage of being "lighter" in a society where skin tone can be a determiner of fate. Imagine being a big black boy who can barely read and write and who gets a constant preparatory beating not only by the system of segregation but by the system that is supposed to be educating him. Can you imagine such a man-child venturing through the racism inherent from the moment he stepped aboard that dilapidated bus, rode past the modern and equipped white school to his own three-room wooden building complete with a water pump and an outhouse? He was unable to utilize white children's cast off textbooks that his family could not afford to purchase, so he had to share with someone else, with the only opportunities to garner attention being his own sexual displays or success at the end of the whip. How different was the end of that whip from the end of a hangman's noose or the end of a police officer's revolver?

We stayed in Halifax, Virginia, for most of that year. We loved it! We were able to experience four distinct seasons replete with snow.

We understood what the term *fall* meant when those beautiful walnut, hickory, birch and oak trees dropped their leaves. We had seen pine cones before, but never like the ones that are native to the state of Virginia. We spent our summer days feeding tobacco worms to hungry chickens, catching fireflies, wading in the creek, and batting with June bugs as if they were baseballs. Those large bugs flew so slowly that we could walk backwards and still walk faster than the loud insects could fly. The grandparents' place in rural Halifax had a well in the backyard and an outhouse farther south, near the hog pen. We experienced Grandma making lye soap, yeast rolls, butter, and fresh fried chicken. I was horrified to learn that you had to kill a live chicken to get fried chicken. I thought that you only had to buy a package of chicken parts from Safeway. That fall, Junior and I pretended to be sick so that we could stay home from school and see a real live hog killing. The sounds of the hogs squealing silenced by the blasts from the shotgun made us shiver with fear. We dared not to go down to the hog pen to watch, but we could smell! Grandpa and the men tied the hogs up by their feet and first slit their throats then their abdomens! The smell of warm hog blood was never to be forgotten by us. Nor were we to ever forget the smell that emitted from the slain hogs when their abdomens were cut and all of their innards fell out into large galvanized tubs. Grandma and the women had set up a large kettle further down toward the creek, and they used the boiling water to pour through the intestines for the first cleaning. That boiling water pushed the fecal matter out, but the women then had to spend hours with paring knives, pulling the fat away from the intestines, and boy did that fat stink! All that work and stink for chitterlings? They were hardly worth it! The hogs were butchered; and the hams, hocks, and what would eventually become bacon were hung with care in the smokehouse. The hair and bristles were scraped off, and the resulting skin was deep fried into "skins." The best parts of the hog were cut up into ribs, loin roasts, and steaks. Nothing was thrown away. The feet were boiled down with vinegar and spices and then canned. The tongue was boiled, stripped, and served as a luncheon meat. The ears, lips, tails, and snouts along with whatever flesh was left on the head was simmered down with a ton of spices and vinegar. The gelatinous mixture was cooled and served with crackers as the delicacy known as hog head cheese.

Junior and I were the smartest kids at the little three-room country school. That was one of the reasons that Mommy decided to take us back to California. Mommy remembered the plan that she and her husband had for their children—to educate them in the state of California.

Another reason why she decided to take us back to California was our father, Cleophus Duarté himself. He had been writing to her about his experiences with the hospital and his experiences with his own personal doctor as an outpatient. He was feeling better, and he was routinely doing his exercises and taking his medicine and vitamins. He claimed that he missed her and the children, and he wanted them all to be a family again. He told her how he had cultivated a vegetable garden in the backyard and how he had planted some pretty flowers in the front yard. Oh, and he was cutting the front lawn every Saturday morning like clockwork. He had signed a contract to get the 1960 edition of the *Encyclopedia Britannica* complete with the atlas for the children as soon as it was released. He wanted his children to have the benefit of their own set of encyclopedias in the home for their studies. He had opened a new bank account, and he had included her name on it. She just needed to sign the signature cards when she returned. He was starting to sound like the man she had left her first husband for.

The ultimate reason that she decided to take us back to California was the fight she had with Grandma. The preacher and his family were coming over for dinner one Sunday. As was tradition, the big table was set in the parlor for the adults, and the children's table was set up in the kitchen. Mommy had started to fix the children's plates when Grandma admonished her and demanded that she stop immediately.

"You know the children don't eat until after the guests have eaten. Put that food back in those pots. Those children can wait."

"No, Mom. My children cannot wait. You used to do that to us when we were coming up. We'd be setting around hungry, waiting for the adults to finish eating before we could eat. They always ate the best pieces of chicken, leaving us the necks and the backs. The mashed potatoes, gravy, and biscuits would be cold, and the ice would be melted in the lemonade. No! Junior likes the thigh. Cleodine and Karol Ann like the drumsticks. Reverend Pryor's children told me that they favor the wings. I am going to feed the children first, and then they can go outside and play while the adults are eating."

"Like hell you will! This is *my* home, and as long as you are in *my* home, you will do what I say!" Grandma had yelled and slammed her fist on the table.

"Then me and my kids will just get out of *your* home. I have my own home to go to, and my children will get to eat there like they are somebody—not like they are one of the barn animals."

The Halifax chapter was ended the following week. Mommy packed all three of us up and moved back to California to where our father appeared happy to see us. He was there at the Greyhound Bus Station to pick us up as soon as the bus pulled into the terminal. He had filled the refrigerator and freezer with food the day before we arrived. Everything in the home was neat and orderly. The front lawn was cut. There were a few flower plants straining to survive along the side of the house, and the backyard garden consisted of three stalks of corn. Everyone was home again.

CHAPTER 17

Aurora

THERE IS THAT DELICATE REALM of enchantment and fascination that children reside in until "that day."

The days before were filled with gentle awakenings, warm oatmeal, hot chocolate, grilled cheese sandwiches with tomato soup, Hostess CupCakes, Mickey Mouse, Donald Duck and Elmer Fudd, play dates, warm baths and warm pajamas and slippers prior to being tucked into a warm bed, being read to and kissed good-night. When they had they chest colds, I gave them orange juice, hot chicken soup, cups of hot Dr. Pepper over slices of lemon, and Vicks VapoRub rubbed onto their chests and covered with a warm cloth at night. They peeked out of the window at night, and they saw stars and the moon. They wondered, "Is the moon really made of green cheese? Will we ever get to see a real Martian?" They played jump rope, hopscotch, marbles, and four square ... softball, kickball, tether ball. They also rode bikes, played with dolls, pretended to be Superman and tried to jump successfully off fences. They captured polliwogs and watched them grow into frogs, and they sprinkled salt onto snails to watch them dissolve. They came home tearfully with skinned knees, splinters, and tummy aches. They were nurtured, guided, provided for, and loved daily. Innocence and trust enveloped them as the beauty and fragrance of roses enveloped the gardener standing outside after a soft rain. As children, they fluttered through their daily routines as butterflies fluttered through the sun-kissed garden—no premonitions of darkness, dangers, or uncertainty. Then for the first time, the muffled sounds they thought they heard while dreaming became a stark reality. On that day, they witnessed the person who was supposed to love and protect us all, their father, hit the person who physically and emotionally nurtured and took care of them—me. And they have heard me cry out.

I wanted Duarté to be embraced by the sense of a good home: soft clean towels trifolded on the racks in the bathroom, fresh flowers from the garden in alabaster vases, lemon 7 Up pound cake cooling on the kitchen windowsill, the aroma permeating every room of the home, and his favorite dinner—fried calf's liver smothered in brown gravy with onions, rice, turnip greens with rutabagas, honey corn (a sweet corn soufflé), and hot water cornbread. I had the radio on, and Dave Brubeck was playing. How he loved Dave Brubeck! I hoped that my attention to each of the five senses would combine to alter the mood that usually entered the home when *he* entered.

When Duarté was home, he found fault with everything and everyone. The venetian blinds were not clean and sanitized. The garbage can wasn't lined correctly. I had not cleaned the linoleum in the kitchen appropriately because he could discover caked-up dirt in the corners. His khakis were not starched and ironed correctly. Once, he had taken a load of freshly ironed clothing, examined them, and thrown them into the bathtub and then filled the tub with water—admonishing me with a facial slap and directions to "do them over." The beatings were not as frequent as they had been. I had learned how to avoid his anger. Do not open the mail. Do not throw away food. Do not overspend at the grocery store. Do not leave the beds unmade. Do not spend too much time on the telephone. Do not associate with Mrs. Do, the Korean neighbor who lived down the alley, or Mrs. Freilich, the German neighbor who lived next door. They were Gooks and Krauts, and all they wanted to do was to find out what he was doing. Duarté would be home soon, and everything would be just perfect.

The evening went well. He had enjoyed his dinner and the ambience of all the sensual stimulators I had employed. Uh-oh! Those kids! There were problems after that perfect dinner! Junior's teacher had called to say that he had been late to school again that morning. "What do you mean by *again?*" he implored. Junior tried to explain that he was late to class because he had to go to the restroom to do number 2. He always waited until everyone had left the public restroom so that he could be alone. It usually happened after he had walked to school each morning. "I can't help it, Daddy," Junior had tried to explain. "There is no such word as *can't* in this house!" he had shouted at our son. Cleodine had to produce her arithmetic test, and she had only earned a C+.

"We don't accept anything lower than an A in this house!" he had shouted. "If you earn less than an A, you have not learned the material, and that is unacceptable!"

"But, Daddy, I can't do all those problems that she gives us."

"There is no such word as *can't* in this house!" he had shouted at her.

"Aurora, what in hell do you do all day that these children are late to school *again* and are not getting As on arithmetic tests?"

After whipping the kids for their insolence, he turned to me and told me that we would talk later after the kids had gone to bed.

I lengthened that time interval as long as I could, nurturing the kids with long baths (forcing him to relieve himself outside against the garage), taking special pains to clean the kitchen thoroughly, scrubbing the floor and corners on my hands and knees, setting the kids' school attire out for the next day, and preparing their lunch bags. I spent extra time soaking in my own bath, anticipating that he might be asleep by the time I retired to the bedroom. No such luck. He was still in the living room, watching the late news when I entered our bedroom through the girls' room. The house was designed so that a person could walk completely through it in a circular fashion. There was a walk-in closet separating the master bedroom from the girls' room. I tiptoed from the bathroom into the kitchen, through the girls' room, the closet, and into our bedroom. I didn't turn on the light; I didn't need it. I could sense the pink-and-red-rose-patterned wallpaper, the dresser, the chair, and the bed with a white chenille bedspread. I slipped into the bed quietly and tried to be asleep when he entered. I heard the "Star-Spangled Banner" playing on the TV announcing the end of programming for the evening. He allowed the song to finish and only got up to turn off the set when the monotone hum began. I thought that I heard him and Stuart talking about the news, but Stuart must have tired and gone home while I was soaking in the bathtub.

It was after midnight at that time, and Cleodine was awakened by the sounds of me sobbing and begging Duarté to "please stop." There were intermittent sounds of furniture crashing, dishes breaking, and a human body (mine) being slammed into a wall and onto the floor. Cleodine got up and ran to the doorway between the bedroom that she shared with Karol Ann and the kitchen. The room was a mess! The table and two chairs were overturned, and there were tufts of brown fuzzy balls on the floor. When she saw her father dragging me across the floor by my hair, she recognized the fuzzy tufts as hair that had been pulled from my head! I was crying and pleading, "Duarté, please," to no avail. Cleodine ran up to him, didn't dare touch him, but yelled at him to "Leave my mother alone!" He simply slung her against the wall and continued his relentless attack on me. Cleodine picked up the telephone, called the operator, and cried, "Help, my father is trying to kill us!"

When she came to, she was sitting on the floor with her back against the wall. The telephone cord had been yanked from the wall, and the telephone was lying on the floor near her. He was sitting in the big chair, wearing his reading glasses, smoking a filterless Pall Mall cigarette and reading the *Wall Street Journal* upside down, oblivious to the evidence of physical assault scattered around him. A broken lamp, upturned chairs, torn bathrobe, clotted blood, and my hair in tufts scattered around the floor of the living room and kitchen. The doorbell rang. Stuart, who was standing unobservable in the shadows, did not get up to answer, and Duarté didn't answer it either. There were knocks, and Duarté still did not answer. The police officers entered the house through the backdoor. When he had slammed the telephone against the head of our oldest daughter, I had first run to her. Seeing that she was unconscious, I picked her up, placed her in a sitting position against the wall, and then had run through the backdoor to the Freilich house to call for help. I am certain that Stuart had to have seen the whole thing, but he was never one to meddle into someone else's marital affairs. His only purpose for being was to advise Cleophus when he was confused.

"Sir, can you tell us what happened here?" the police queried Duarté.

He answered "Nothing. I have been sitting here reading my own self newspaper, minding my self-business like you should be doing."

Noticing the officer purveying the destruction in the room, he recalled the wisdom of Scripture, his father, and succinctly continued with his monologue in the manner that he had been taught: "This is my own self property, my own self house, and this is my own self family. If I choose to be the man of my house that I bought and paid cash for, and discipline my wife and family, that is my own self business as well."

He took two long drags off that filterless Pall Mall and continued reading his newspaper as Stuart guardedly watched everything and everyone. The police took Duarté and his newspaper that night. My victimized daughter prayed to God that he would never come back. The other three children seemingly slept through everything and couldn't remember even hearing any of the fracas. The truth was, Junior had heard it, and he had deliberately covered his head with his pillow to shut it out. What was he supposed to do? Interfere with his father disciplining his mother? Could he stand to look into my eyes seeing my tearful hurt and do nothing? It was easier to just stay asleep.

That delicate realm of enchantment and fascination that children reside in until "that day" is sometimes compared with the rose-colored glasses that can mask the abusive nature of a marital mate until "that day" reveals the truth to everyone.

The Vallejo Police Department took Duarté with them that night, and he willingly let them cuff and place him in the back seat of the police vehicle. I was working at the sewing factory when he appeared at the home the next morning to tell the kids goodbye and to get Beneva, the babysitter, to iron a shirt for him.

"I am sick, and I am going to get some help," he had told them as he climbed into the waiting taxicab. "Beneva, please give this to Aurora and tell her that I will call her." He handed Beneva a one-hundred-dollar bill.

"Wow!" the children had exclaimed. They each wanted to touch it, put it up to their faces, sniff it, and pretend to put it into their respective pockets. They had never seen a hundred-dollar bill before. They never saw their father again after that day. I never saw the hundred-dollar bill entrusted to Beneva either.

Chapter 18

Cleodine

Even though our father never came back to live with the family, Junior inherited the passion to control females by demonstrating force with tactics to arouse mortal fear in his victim. Years later, his timid wife had threatened to kill herself, and he had driven her out to the dock of the bay, invited her to walk out into the water until it was neck high, and then he had fired a pistol over her head. When the police questioned him, he claimed that the pistol was only a relay pistol and that he was "teaching her a lesson" for threatening to end her life. She had walked out into the bay of her own accord, and he was admonishing her for her absurdity. He was her husband. She was his own self wife, and he had the right to discipline her.

I vowed never to let a man beat me the way my father had beaten my mother. The day I walked down the aisle to marry, I took those precious steps with the resolution in the forefront of my mind that I would not have to stay in the relationship if my husband should attempt to physically abuse me. I had my own self house, my own self job, my own self degrees, and my own self family. I was definitely prepared to make it without him. Decades later, the man I had married went to his grave with two visible areas of keloidal scar tissue: a small wound to his left cheek and a three-inch wound to his right forearm, both obtained when he unsuccessfully attempted to physically discipline me, his own self wife, for daring to complain about his nocturnal absences.

No, my father never came back to the family. He faithfully sent money each month for a few years, and then he stopped altogether. When Mommy threatened to contact the USAF about his lack of financial support, he threatened to kill her. His money was his own self money, and she had better not try to take even one penny of it. While he was sending the money, Mommy was able to support the family on what he sent, the lower prices at the commissary, and from what she earned as a seamstress. This also allowed her to stay at home with her children. We had hot breakfasts each day except for Saturday when we could eat cold cereal. We had hot lunches each school day when we came home for lunch. We had sandwiches and mugs of hot soup packed in our lunchboxes on cold and rainy days when we didn't need to be out in the elements more than necessary. We attended Sunday school and morning worship service each week along with Baptist Training Union (BTU), choir rehearsal, and whatever children's program was in process. We were well known at school and highly respected because we each read several grade levels above our respective ages, and Junior was an absolute whiz in math. We participated in Cub Scouts, Brownies, and Girl Scouts, Little League Baseball, and marbles tournaments. We rode bicycles all over the place. When he stopped sending money, Mommy took a full-time position at a factory that made doll clothing. To supplement her earnings, she cleaned house for a Chinese physician, and she still did sewing when she had the time. It seemed to me that we rarely saw her anymore. She was always either sleeping, getting ready to go to work, or coming home from work dead tired. Mother Beatrice took up the slack and routinely picked us up for BTU, choir rehearsal, and even church on Sundays.

I remember that Junior had never really been a protector for me. How unlike his father who as a youth growing up in Mississippi would protect his little sister, Melody, not only from the older siblings but anyone else who would even think about trying to harm her. Junior did not protect me against Willie when we were in Halifax. Junior did not protect me against Big Lucy when we lived in Floyd Terrace, and I learned to avoid the nasty Floyd Terrace boys who would exhibit the same sexual assaults as Willie should they come upon a girl alone. Could be because Junior did not have a strong father figure like Scripture Duarté to guide him as he grew into manhood.

Junior began to exhibit the maniacal tendencies like our father around the age of fourteen. He became incorrigible, yelling at Mommy, hitting me in my face, stealing money from Mommy, and even threatening to hit her. About this time, he began his in and out relationship with the juvenile authorities as well. Very intelligent yet easily bored with the mundane, he was arrested for building a raft and sailing across Lake Chadwyck. He had remembered the exploits of Huckleberry Finn, and he wanted to experience the thrills that Huck had experienced. He was given an IQ test in juvenile hall, which he aced, and he was sent home. He was far too intelligent to be in the facility with the rest of the boys who routinely ended up there. The second time he got into trouble, he had hopped onto a locomotive engine, started it, and had actually driven it a mile before he was stopped. He was given an IQ test in juvenile hall, which he aced, and he was sent home. He was far too intelligent to be in the facility with the rest of the boys who routinely ended up there. The pattern repeated itself over and over again.

The husband of Miz Birdie, Mommy's best friend, routinely included Junior in outings with his own son, and the two boys became very close friends. But as they grew older, Junior developed into one type of person as Billy developed into another. By high school, they were still friends but rarely shared the same experiences as they had as children. Billy was part of a band named Project Soul that eventually developed into the world-renown band Confunction. Billy went on to college to major in music and spent his professional life teaching music for the Oakland Unified School District. Junior made his mark gambling, drinking, dealing drugs, and racing cars and motorcycles. As he grew into manhood without a father of his own to guide him, Junior's first offenses were more out of boredom and curiosity than malice. He flirted with shoplifting bicycle parts, sneaking into movie theaters, speeding, and deliberately running red lights.

He dropped out of high school and immediately went to work first at Port Chicago and later at the Mare Island Naval Shipyard.

Without a high school diploma, he was able to pass entrance examinations that engineers struggled with. He was hired but not as an engineer. In some cases, his responsibility was to train the newly graduated engineer recruits. He was paid well for his expertise, but not as much as those he trained. In retaliation, he would go to work and deliberately take long breaks, a long lunch, and long naps. His argument was that he could do in four hours what took the white boys eight hours to complete. He was fired. He filed a lawsuit, became disenchanted with his attorney, fired him, and represented himself. He argued his own case against the team of attorneys sent in from Washington DC, and he prevailed. He was awarded his job back, his back pay, and the pay differential between what he had been earning and what his white counterparts had been earning. He celebrated by buying a new red motorcycle that he nicknamed the Red Ninja, new clothes, loaned his drinking buddy's money, and he threw a victory party for himself with plenty of liquor for everyone. He went to work that Monday drunk, fell asleep on the job and was fired again. This time, the termination stuck.

The first time he did any real hard time came about when he test-drove a car and did not bring it back. He was caught, arrested, given a jail sentence, and let out on probation. While on probation, he did the same thing with a motorcycle. It took the police nearly a month to catch up with him and that motorcycle, but when they did, he was arrested again. Since he was already on probation, the judge gave him a stiffer sentence—he was sent to the California State Prison System at San Luis Obispo. That particular prison was considered the country club of prisons. It housed educated and nonviolent white-collar criminals who enjoyed a variety of privileges that illiterate and violent inmates in the other state prisons did not have access to. Junior felt like he was in heaven. He had a television and radio in his cell (paid for by Mommy). There were all sorts of activities that the prisoners could partake of: softball, tennis, swimming, billiards, weight lifting, horseback riding, culinary arts, horticulture, garment design, painting, auto mechanics, track and field, and accredited college classes. It was like they were in a private prep school as opposed to a prison. Junior lost his opportunity to bask in that environment when he refused to mop a floor as ordered.

"I don't mop nobody's floor!" he had told them. The prison authorities didn't argue the matter with him.

"Fine. Then we will put you someplace where all you have to do is sit on your ass in your cell all day."

He was transferred to San Quentin. That was the last time that he had to do hard time in a California State Prison. Mommy, brokenhearted, spent tens of thousands of dollars on lawyer and legal fees to finally get him out on parole. He had called her begging and crying. Just as she was gullible to our father's pleadings for "another chance," she was gullible to her son's pleas for help.

Chapter 19

Cleodine

Junior and I had been so close as young siblings. I was perplexed when he started to change toward me. When we were small, we played together every day, and we shared everything. We shared a bedroom in those early days, and we could barely wait for the lights to go out so that we could embark upon our favorite game of "combat." Each of us had stored a bastion of rolled-up socks under our respective pillows. At night, we would each pull the top edge of the bedspread up over the top of the headboard, thus making a military tent. From these tents, we would throw the sock bombs at each other, scoring a hit when a sock bomb made contact with the other sibling's body.

As he entered puberty, Junior continued to digress into a person the entire house was afraid of. He stole money from Mommy's purse, stole my lunch money, yelled back at Mommy, slapped me in the face whenever I made him angry, and cut school whenever he felt like it. The home on Alameda Street was destroyed by fire—a fire accidently set by Junior. His junior high school was on double sessions, so he didn't leave for school until ten o'clock each morning. He had been making and flying paper airplanes in the house when he decided to make some dive bombers. He lit the tail ends of several paper planes and was flying them throughout the house when one of them landed on top of a box of dress patterns. The box exploded into flames. Frightened, Junior ran outside and hid in some bushes down the alley. By the time the fire department, less than a block away, saw the flames coming from the roof, the home was engulfed.

I was in the sixth grade when the family moved to the Floyd Terrace Projects as a result of the fire that destroyed the home on Alameda Street. It took Mommy a whole year to move the family out of the projects because *he* would not sign the papers that would allow her to either rebuild the house or sell the property. The city of Vallejo eventually took the property as an eyesore and gave Mommy what they "claimed" was market value for it. Until that time, we had to live and survive in the Floyd Terrace Projects. I had to fend for myself against the nasty boys like Leonard Venue, who would walk through the projects singing in a loud voice, "Beat on your meaty meat! Beat! Beat! Beat on your meaty meat!" I also had to fend for myself against bullies like Big Lucy. The Floyd Terrace children who lived on the upper end of East Lane attended Cooper Elementary School in the white area of town. We had to walk through a white neighborhood to reach the ten-foot-high drainage pipe that separated white Vallejo from the Floyd Terrace Projects.

"You think you're something because yo mama got a job!"

Those words were the precursor to the daily poundings that I received from the menace to society named Big Lucy. She was thirteen, weighed close to two hundred pounds, had red nappy hair and a freckled face. Most of the afterschool fights took place in the drainage pipes out of sight of any adults, but Big Lucy assaulted me during the first block of our trek home. She would walk up to me from behind and just slam me in the back with her fists until I fell to the ground. If I tried to run, Big Lucy would just catch me and slam me a few more times. In the projects, if Big Lucy caught me outside, she would slap me hard in the face at least once. It seemed that she needed to daily hit me as badly as some adults needed to have a daily cup of coffee in the morning or a cigarette after dinner. Mommy tried to reason with Big Lucy's mother, but that lady threatened to slap Mommy if she didn't mind her own business. "Kids is kids, and they will work it all out," she had said. The school administration claimed they could not do anything since the alleged attacks did not take place on the school grounds. When I became a professional educator myself, I learned that this was just a put-off. The school has jurisdiction over a student from the time that student leaves home en route to school until that student returns. The school authorities just did not want to intervene in a combative situation involving the Negro children from the Floyd Terrace Projects. Their lack of concern and involvement was like how people sometimes put salt on a snail. Put enough salt on it, and it will disappear. When asked, Big Lucy would always say that I was the one who had attacked her without reason, and that was enough to satisfy the school authorities. They did nothing to intervene. The daily beatings continued.

I recognized some of the same behavioral characteristics that I had experienced in Halifax County. There were Negro children who despised themselves, their way of life, and those Negro children who did not fit in with them. Most of the children who resided on East Lane were from single-parent households. Each of these households contained children, most of whom had different and absent fathers, and were maintained with County Welfare allotments. On the days that the welfare lady came to visit, the children were scrubbed clean, the dismal apartments were scrubbed clean, sprayed for cockroaches, and any items that had been purchased from the "hot" truck (toasters, television sets, radios, record players, new irons, and bottles of liquor) were carefully hidden from view. Welfare boxes were received monthly and the contents shared (butter, bricks of processed cheese, apples, oranges, pears, flour, sugar, and peanut butter). Most of the children were behind at least one year in school. They blamed the white teachers for deliberately flunking the colored children, but when I sat in class with these children, I could understand why they had been retained.

By the time I started the seventh grade, Solano JHS had opened, and the students from Floyd Terrace were assigned to attend. It was quite a trek to get to school, at least one hour walk for those who could not afford to take the city bus. Even at a fare of only ten cents each way, taking the bus each day did not leave much left over for lunch for children from impoverished households. To add insult to injury, the Vallejo Unified School District provided free school bus transportation for the white students who lived in College Park and attended Solano JHS. Now, the College Park homes were less than a twenty-minute walk from Solano JHS. Colored students walking for an hour or more from the Floyd Terrace Projects passed by that segregated housing development on their way to and from school each day. I remembered the white student school bus from Halifax County as I saw the VUSD bus loaded with white students pass by while we were walking. Attempts to get the school district to provide bussing for the Floyd Terrace Project students were futile. Thus, the Negro children took their anger out on the white students who were able to ride to school while they were relegated to walking. You might call it poetic justice—the way the Negro walkers violated the rights of the white bus riders. They had learned their lessons well from the televised reports of the civil rights struggles in the south and the attempt to integrate schools in Little Rock, Arkansas. Voter registration buses were overturned and burned. Voter registration workers (black and white) were targeted, beaten, jailed, and in some cases, murdered. Negro children being bused to predominantly white schools feared for their lives when the anger of the whites was visited upon them. Some of the displays of white anger included the physical attack on school buses, rocks and sticks thrown, vicious beatings of the students, and terror in the hallways of the once all-white school campuses. I saw firsthand a remake of the violence—Vallejo style. There were rocks thrown at the school bus, white students pummeled with fists in the hallways, lunch trucks robbed of the overpriced junk food that they were selling to students, and blatant disrespect toward the white teachers who appeared to favor the white students over the black. It was terrible! The self-hatred was so evident. I still get sick when I think of Melita, the Negro girl who never had a lunch nor lunch money. On a daily basis, she would come to a group of students and ask for a "bite" of everyone's sandwich or a "sip" of their soda. A group of filthy Negro boys played the most disgusting trick on Melita. Sick of her "begging" during lunch, one of them urinated into a half-filled bottle of Royal Crown Cola. When Melita appeared to routinely ask for a "bite" or a "sip," this bottle was presented to her.

"You can have the whole thing. I'm finished with it," that infidel said to her. Melita took two long swigs of the soda before she started to gag.

"It tastes like dog piss!" she exclaimed.

Those boys fell to the ground, laughing at her.

"No, it's not dog piss. It is Nigga piss, and you just drank it, you beggin'-assed bitch."

To make matters worse that tumultuous year, my first-period class was home economics, the required elective for all seventh-grade female students. Each seventh-grade girl would be assigned to a semester of culinary arts and a semester of clothing construction. I was all settled into my table group when Big Lucy came in with a schedule change. She was moving from the sixth-period class to the first-period class, and she was assigned to sit at the same four-student kitchen as me! For the first two weeks of school, I endured the kicks to my shins under the table and the punches in the back in the hallway all deftly delivered by Big Lucy. My request to move to a different kitchen was denied by the teacher. My request to move to a different class period was denied by the counselor. I dared not tell anyone at the office that Big Lucy was assaulting me because the walk home to Floyd Terrace was so long, there was no telling what Big Lucy would do to me, and experience at Cooper Elementary School had taught me that the school authorities would do nothing about it. So I remained quiet and just took it. That is, until the day that Big Lucy arrived at school one morning with an attitude nastier than any that I had ever seen before. In addition to slamming me in the back, Big Lucy had slapped me in the face right before we entered the classroom. When I got up to sharpen my pencil, Big Lucy had deliberately tripped me and laughed out loud when I fell on my face in front of the entire classroom. Seated, Big Lucy had continued the assault on my shins, and when I did not cry, Big Lucy devised another form of treachery. She pretended to be writing in her journal, but she was saying out loud what she was pretending to write: "Somebody at this table has a momma who is a ho. She thinks she is so much more than the rest of us because her momma puts on a nurse's uniform every day and pretends to go to work in the hospital. But everybody knows that her children are all by different men, and she really is a ho working down at the waterfront."

The next thing that I knew was that I had slapped Big Lucy so hard across the face that she fell down on her fat backsides to the floor. They say that I jumped on top of her and pummeled her face with my fists and grabbed her hair with both hands.

"Say something else about my momma, say it and eat your breakfast in hell tomorrow morning!" I reportedly screeched as I banged her head against the linoleum floor.

They say that when they finally pulled me from Big Lucy, I had tufts of her hair in both hands, and hair roots could be seen dangling from some of it. It took three teachers to pull us apart. Witnesses say that I was blabbering, stuttering, and still trying to punch Big Lucy while the latter was crying and wiping snot with the sleeve of her sweater. Both of us were suspended from school for three days for the incident which was deemed to be a mutual combat. That night, Mommy tore my backsides up for allowing myself to be manipulated into such unseemly behavior in school. I was not being sent there to fight. I was being sent there to get an education.

"There is nothing that anyone can say to you about me or any other member of the family that will give you license to act like that. You have to be above that type of uncivilized behavior. It better not happen again."

It did not happen again. The word got out in the projects that Cleodine Duarté had gone crazy and kicked Big Lucy's butt in front of the whole class. Big Lucy never put a hand on me again. I basked in the well of respect that I had finally earned in the projects. I never had to fight at that school again.

It was more than three decades later when I learned the sad story about Big Lucy. The brother of Big Lucy's grandfather was her biological father. She had come to being due to an incestuous rape that had gone unpunished. Her ravaged fourteen-year-old mother was actually chastised for wearing tight short pants in the presence of this "uncle" whom everyone knew was an alcoholic who was out of control when he drank. When Big Lucy's family got together for holidays, her biological father would come with his white woman on his arm, eat up dinner that her mother had helped to prepare, drink up liquor, cheat at cards, and then roll away in his shiny new Cadillac. The year that Big Lucy was seven, her mother had asked this uncle/daddy for money to purchase a bicycle for their daughter. He had hemmed and hawed before stating that he didn't have any extra cash this time but would see about getting the bicycle next time. The following week, he had driven up to the family Christmas dinner in a new Cadillac, and his new white woman was brandishing a new fur coat and a new pair of diamond earrings. Big Lucy's mother had blasted through the passenger window of the new Cadillac and punched that white woman in the face with her fist, knocking out two of her front teeth before the uncle/daddy pummeled her with his fists prior to driving away all the time cussing at her for the lack of respect to his woman.

Big Lucy had three other siblings, all fathered by different men, and it was rumored that her mother worked down on the waterfront. What an unhappy child she must have been. Her attacks on me were actually attacks upon the aspects of her own life that she deplored. How unfortunate that she never learned how to analyze the situation, develop and implement a plan to remove herself from it, thus protecting her offspring from a repeat of her inherited sadness.

Big Lucy died at the age of twenty-one. She had an appointment for a root canal, and she was deathly afraid that the pain would be unbearable. To ease what could have been an unforgettable and unbearable experience, she had prepared herself for the ordeal by consuming Johnny Walker Red Label whiskey, and she popped a few reds for good measure. That mixture seemed to ignite when the dentist administered the anesthesia, and her heart stopped—forever.

Chapter 20

Cleo

THE YEAR THAT I TURNED thirteen was a year of reality and a year of changes. Mommy had studied for and passed the state board exam and became a registered nurse. With the promotion from the salary of the LVN to the salary of the RN, one would think that things would get better. She began to volunteer for the night shift because there was a pay differential, and the patients tended to sleep throughout the night. Most of the night nurses stretched their duties out as long as they could, appearing to be busy, but after making her rounds and completing her paperwork, Mommy could settle down in a comfortable chair and finish hemming some garments that she was making for one of her daughters, herself, or some lady at church. She knitted, crocheted, hemmed garments, and covered buttons, handbags and shoes at night—thus earning some extra money.

That was the year that four little black girls lost their lives while attending Sunday school in Birmingham, Alabama. I watched helplessly as Mommy shed tears while reading the newspaper accounting of the church bombing. Eight weeks later, President John F. Kennedy was assassinated on live television! It seemed as if the whole world stood still in disbelief and in mourning. The youth that Junior hung out with began to chant their communal disassociation with anything and anyone declared by them to be "the establishment."

"If they will blow up a church to kill little black girls and kill a white president—all in broad daylight—what do you think they will do to me?" they chanted. "Nothing if I get to them first." Thus, began a series of white-versus-black gang fights after school and on the weekends. Junior fought against some of the same white boys he had ridden bicycles with, played marbles with, and served in the Cub Scouts with. They became the Greys while his soul brothers became My People.

I was also changing. I rebelled against wearing the saddle oxfords that had been a staple of my school wardrobe ever since I started school. I wanted to wear flats and maybe even high heels to school. Mommy would not hear of it, so I took to hiding a pair of patent leather flats in a set of bushes a couple of doors away from home. I would change shoes on the way to school and again on the way back home. The long walk to the junior high school was devastating to those flats, and I learned to keep the flats in my locker and wear my PE shoes to and from school for the long walk.

I also rebelled against my name, Cleodine Georgette Duarté. "It sounds like Farmer John's cow!" I complained to Mommy, who would not hear of a legal name change.

"We gave you the name Cleodine, and that is the name you are going to keep until you are grown and in a house of your own. Then you can do what you want with your name."

"But why Cleodine?"

"Your father wanted you to have part of his name, that is why."

"But Karol Ann and Luther don't have part of his name. They have normal people names. Why didn't he give them atrocious names as well?"

"He was away in the Air Force when each of them was born, and he wasn't in a position to come home. You and Junior named Karol Ann. Your father wanted to call her Cleophette Geneva, but he wasn't here to enforce his wishes. He wanted to call Luther, Cleotis Gregory, but he wasn't here then either. Mom picked his name."

"Lucky buttholes."

Aurora turned around toward her eldest daughter, ready to whack the daylights out of her. "What did you say?"

"Nothing."

My friend Katherine had adopted the nickname of Kitty. Her friend Wilhelmina had adopted the nickname of Willie. Cassandra had become Sandy. Patricia had become Pat. Delores had become Dee. That year, I adopted the nickname of Cleo, and it stuck from that point on.

CHAPTER 21

Butt Whooping Saturday

THAT AFTERNOON, THE JACKSON KIDS were going to get butt whoopings from their father. This sort of quarterly ritual took place on a Saturday afternoon after all the kids' chores had been completed, Mrs. Jackson had left to go make groceries, and Mr. Jackson was awakened, cleansed, fed, and sobered up from the night before. He saved up butt whooping tokens like children saved up 7 Up bottle caps, For the children, their prize at the end of the tunnel was a free movie at the Crown Theater on a Saturday afternoon. For their daddy, his prize was the sight of those seven squirming and bleeding behinds laid out at his disposal. Yes, he was the man of his house— or so he perceived. His house was actually a composite of one and one-third project apartments with the adjoining wall knocked out (a three-bedroom with an additional bedroom). His "house" consisted of four bedrooms, a living room, an eat-in kitchen, and one bathroom. The Housing Authority allowed larger families to accommodate the larger living spaces, so with a family of nine, he was living high on the projects' hog.

The butt-whooping tokens were saved up in what must have been an imaginary jar at the base of his head, and when he felt there were enough tokens to validate the time and energy it took to administer the punishments, he laid them out. He kept tokens for notes home from the teachers, squirming during the Sunday sermon at church, coming home late from school, failing a spelling test, talking back to an adult, not taking the garbage out without being told, taking too long in the bathroom, arguing with siblings, fighting over toys, letting an outsider beat up a sibling, not cleaning their plates during a meal, complaining about what the meal consisted of, looking at him the wrong way, making too much noise … You name the offense, and their daddy tucked them away in that imaginary jar until butt-whooping Saturday.

The other kids in the projects could always tell when butt-whooping Saturday was here. Everyone could hear him in the morning when he viciously slapped Mrs. Jackson upside her head and yelled at her, "Get out of my face, I got some things to do today. You let these damn kids run all over you, but they not going to run all over me."

Mr. Jackson was quite loud. Everyone in the building could hear him when he had sexual relations with his wife. The headboard banged violently against the wall with every thrust, the springs squeaked, and he grunted like a grizzly bear when his appetite had been satiated. Everyone could also hear when he slapped her around. A loud smack followed by the sound of her body falling against the wall or against a piece of furniture was the most common sound because Mrs. Jackson never cried out. She just took it in silence. The children were a different story, and that was why the Upper East Lane children would gather around the base of the Jackson's upstairs bedroom whenever butt-whooping Saturday was here.

Mr. Jackson would start by taking about forty minutes to cleanse his colon, grunting as though he was working on a railroad. The window to the bathroom was open, and the horrific odor floated about like a fog. He must have had a heavy load to unleash because he routinely flushed the toilet every ten to twelve minutes. His children would come downstairs and ask to use the neighbor's bathroom while their daddy was tying up theirs. After the colon-cleansing routine was completed, he would slam around in the kitchen, demanding that his wife fix him something to eat. She could never fix it fast enough, and it was never good enough, because after he had eaten, he would throw his plate in the sink, slap her, and yell at her to get the hell out of there and go make the groceries—and she better not spend all his money. After she had scurried out, he would yell for the kids to get ready. To get ready meant to strip naked and lie down across their parents' bed. The kids would always start to whimper and plead, "Please, Daddy ..." all to no avail. He made the two oldest ones lie on their tummies at the foot of the bed. The next two oldest ones lay on their tummies at the head of the bed. The three little ones lay on their tummies in the middle of the bed. He would conduct his punishment dressed only in his boxer shorts and sleeveless T-shirt. He must not have wanted to get his work clothes or Sunday clothes mussed up from the sweat he was going to develop during his butt-whooping ritual. He had a well-worn leather strap that he used to inflict his punishments on his children, and sometimes, he wet it so that it would sting even more.

He would begin to whoop the children starting with the older ones. They were stronger and would take more of his energy. He laid that strap across their backs, legs, and buttocks over and over again. After he had whipped them about ten times each, he would turn the strap on the three little ones, then back onto the older ones. He whooped them again and again and again and again in this order. They screamed, moaned, cried, and begged for mercy; and the sounds they made seemed to give him more energy to whoop them some more. The neighborhood children hovering under the window outside demonstrated a myriad of reactions. Some sniggled. Some out right laughed. Some had looks of fear on their faces, and some cried. But none of them left their spot of amusement for fear that the spot would be taken by someone else and they would lose out on an opportunity to hear the Jackson children getting their butts whooped. The whooping continued until the children no longer had voices to holler and scream. Their cries reformed into what sounded like faint cow moos. This would be after about ten minutes of lashing with that belt. Mr. Jackson would tell the children to "Shut up or I'll give you something else to cry about."

Then even the mooing would stop, but you could hear the hoarse breathing coming from that bedroom all the way outside. The children hanging around outside would dissipate. No one wanted to be around when Mr. Jackson descended from that apartment!

After a butt whooping, the children missed Sunday school and church service, and they missed school for the following week as well. They seldom came out of the house during the week after a butt whooping unless it was to take out the garbage or take clothes off the clothesline. If someone did get a glimpse of one of them, that person would quickly look away so that they would not be noticed openly staring at the welts and oozing wounds on the exposed legs and arms. God only knows what their backs and buttocks looked like.

*****

The Floyd Terrace Projects were cleared to make room for a new housing development and the upgraded expansion of Kaiser Permanente Hospital. Some of the families relocated to project housing in another locale. Some moved to Country Club Crest, which was fast becoming a major ghetto area complete with drugs, thugs, no public transportation system, Section 8 housing, and lower property values. The Jackson family moved to Alameda County, and the children were seen no more in Vallejo. Word has it that Mr. Jackson eventually lost a battle with colon cancer. Mrs. Jackson eventually lost a battle with breast cancer. The oldest boy hung himself while incarcerated for robbery. The oldest girl received a twenty-seven-year to life sentence for stabbing her mate to death. Two of the boys had been killed in a high-speed chase involving the police. The two youngest had sought careers in the armed services and had never come back to the Bay Area. The middle child has been missing for over two decades.

CHAPTER 22

To Pluck a Ripened Fruit

WHEN MOST PEOPLE HEAR THE word *predator*, they immediately think of an animal that hunts and kills other animals or a deranged human who hunts and kills other humans. There is another type of predator with techniques that are equally as damaging, and unfortunately, some of them are encouraged to demonstrate their techniques by their own fathers.

An infant grows to a toddler to a school-aged child to adolescence to pre-teen and then teenaged years. If during this time of transition from infancy to the interactively subjective world of being a teenager there is no father or other adult male mentor to let a female know that he loves her unconditionally, she is a fruit ripe for plucking by a predator who has been taught to measure his own value by his accomplishments related to "phlucking" virgins. Forgive my version of the vulgar word, but it is an applicable description for what happens. The young female is enraptured by this predator who tells her she is pretty, tells her she is smart and witty, tells her that he loves her above everyone else, tells her that he wants to marry her one day, and he holds her tenderly. He tells her things that replace what her father never has told her, and he expresses physical affection that replace what her father has never expressed. She is so enraptured by his words and his embraces that all she wants to do is to please him. A girl pleases her father by drawing him a picture, baking him a cake, performing a musical number, or bringing home an excellent report card. A girl growing up without a father may please the predator by submitting her virginal body to him. It is painful to her but ultimately pleasing to him. She thinks that she has an endearing love that will be with her for the rest of her life. He, on the other hand, has cut another notch on his belt, and as he is pulling his drawers up, he is thinking about the next ripe plum that he plans to "phluck" before the week is over.

I was fifteen years old, and the person who "phlucked" my virginity was a nineteen-year-old friend of my brother Junior. As Junior had never protected me while we were growing up, he did not protect me from this predator either. In fact, Junior was complicit in the relationship even getting started. Jeremy Edward, also known as Knuckle Head, hung out with Junior. Junior's friends would meet up at our home after Mommy had left for the hospital. They would watch television for a short period, and then they would be off to whatever and wherever their destructives plans could take them. Jeremy Edward would double back to watch television with me so that I would not be "alone" at night. As I look back upon the progression of that relationship now, I see myself as a fifteen-year-old girl whose father had never shown her affection and whose brother would demean and slap her just like she had witnessed her father demean and slap her mother. Jeremy Edward was nice to me. He would hold my hands, hug me, brush my hair, rub my back, and talk to me most of the night—leaving just before Junior would return from his evening's haunts. When I told him about the pregnancy, he had given me a set of diamond wedding rings and said that we would run away together, he would join the Army, and we could raise our child happily.

I conceived in May. He gave me the diamond rings in August. In September, while sitting in my friend's car, preparing to go home from school, a female student approached me with a message from her friend.

"Beulah said for you to give her back her wedding rings, and she wants them today."

"You tell Beulah that I am not going to give her shit! I don't have anything of hers!"

I learned that same week that Jeremy Edward had actually married another girl from the high school named Doretha. Doretha was eighteen and rumored to also be pregnant. When Jeremy Edward came over again, I lit into him with the allegations. In terms of Beulah, he had taken her to her ninth grade prom in June. Beulah had secured some alcohol from her mother's liquor cabinet, and they had both gotten drunk. He did not love her, but he felt obligated to help her because her mother had threatened to kill her, causing Beulah to run away from home. He had hidden her in his parents' home, hiding her under his bed when the parents were home for over a week before discovery. Enraged, Beulah's mother was filing charges against him of statutory rape and contributing to the delinquency of a minor. The attorney that his father had secured had advised him to at least appear to be concerned about what he had done. It would look better if he could show that he wanted to do the "right thing." He claimed that was the reason he had married Doretha. She was also pregnant, and her father had threatened to throw her out of the house if she brought an illegal baby home. The attorney convinced his family that he stood a better chance of staying out of jail if he was married and working full-time. According to him, his family had forced him to marry Doretha to give the child a name and to stay out of jail for the Beulah issue. He planned to divorce Doretha as soon as the child was born so that he and I could be together as man and wife. So he had taken advantage of a gem sale at Gensler and Lee Diamond Store and purchased two identical wedding sets for the price of one with the plan of killing two phlucked birds with one stone, eventually freeing himself to be with the one he claimed he truly loved—me. The set that he had given to me was purchased for Beulah. I gladly gave it back to him, and he promised to get me a new and really expensive set once he got this mess with the other two girls all straightened out.

I began to see him for what he really was—a phlucking fool! I wrote all the facts down on a piece of notebook paper:

- He was nineteen years of age with no high school diploma.
- He only worked sporadically if at all.

- Two additional babies would be born, fathered by him, in the same year as my child.
- He disrespected his own mother just like Junior disrespected Mommy.
- He did not represent the type of role model that I wanted in front of the child I was going to bring into this world.
- When he was not holding me tenderly and lying to me, he was someone that I did not want to be associated with in public.
- He was touted as Baby King of Vallejo, and he reveled in the authentication of what he considered to be his "prowess."
- His father and his uncles appeared to be proud of his accomplishments with the phlucking of fruit. "A chip off the old block," they would boast. "Ain't nothing happy about that boy! No, siree!" The term *happy* was synonymous to the term *gay*. The men in his family were relieved that he phlucked the fruit of females as opposed to other males, so it did not matter that he did so purposefully and irresponsibly.

I determined that Jeremy Edward and all people like him were trash at my feet and would never have an opportunity to hurt me again. Such an individual was someone that I would not even spit on if given the chance. My goals were to finish high school with honors and graduate from college with a BA, MA, and Ph.D. I would get a good professional job; buy my own self house, and raise my own self child. If I married, I would marry someone educated and professional who would love and accept my child, and we would move forward in life like good decent people should.

My pronounced determination saved me from immeasurable pain, anxieties, and horror. That man beat Doretha with his fists while they were living with his parents, while his dear old mom and dad did nothing to intervene. Doretha eventually divorced him and was able to spend the rest of her life in a marital union with a kinder person who loved her and her daughter unconditionally. Jeremy Edward got involved in drug dealing, was caught, turned state witness against the friends he had grown up with and sold drugs with, and suffered an assassination attempt for his efforts. He survived the gunshot wound to his abdomen, and his immediate family had to go into witness protection, Doretha's five-year-old daughter being escorted to and from school by secret service agents to guarantee her safety and his testimony. When it was over, he had to leave the town that he grew up in for his own safety, and when he did, he left a trail of phlucked teenaged fruit that bore his seed annually from the birth of my child who was the first. Aunt Willetta kept count, and she stopped counting at ten. Each of these phlucked teenaged fruits had either an absent father or an abusive father. There was no adult male in the home to express his love and value for either of them. Thus, they each learned to accept what they desired from someone else who was not opposed to deception to reach the desired conquistador-styled objective. Jeremy Edward did not learn much in school other than how to count money. From his father and uncles, he learned how to achieve their respect by the amount of fruit annually phlucked. From the streets, he learned how to live dangerously, wantonly, and insecurely.

As I was maturing, I was learning to choose carefully the individuals who would become a part of my life, how to manage my time and my money, and how to prepare for a future bereft of individuals like Jeremy Edward and Junior Duarté.

Chapter 23

A Courtside Victory

To win at tennis, the player must win with a minimum two-point lead. If the score is tied at 40 to 40 (what is called a deuce), a player must earn two consecutive points (an advantage point and point) to win the game.

Mommy did not play tennis, but the night she confronted me regarding my swelling abdomen, I treated the discourse as a courtside challenge.

She was sitting at her well-utilized Singer sewing machine in the den, glasses on and squinting at the fabric that she was manipulating into some lovely garment. I was sitting in the reclining chair beside her, watching television and enjoying a glass of grape Kool-Aid. I knew instinctively what she was going to ask me before she even opened her mouth.

"Cleodine ..."

"What?" I answered in the most defiant tone I could muster.

"Are you ..." Her voice was too steady and too calm for the volley that was about to take place.

"Am I what? You're always on my case about nothing!" It was her turn to serve, and I had to be on the defensive to send that ball back into a corner of her court that she could not reach.

"I need to know ..." She had stopped sewing, had turned around, and was looking me directly in the face. Oh, I couldn't let her get the advantage over me.

"Need to know what? You don't bother with needing to know about Junior and all the stuff that he is doing. Why are you picking on me? He steals money out of your purse, stays out as late as he wants, and doesn't do any chores. He doesn't even go to school half of the time—and you need to know something about me?" I had the advantage now.

"Are you ..." The tone of her voice had not changed after that last verbal volley. I had to let her know that I still had the advantage.

"What I am is sick and tired of all of this. I wish I had never been born!" That shot should have caused her to stop in her tracks, but it did not.

"Going to have a baby?"? Game point!

"Yes!" Deuce! The next two points will be mine, and I will win!

"Who is the father?"

"I am not going to tell you." Advantage point!

"Go on upstairs and go to bed. We will talk in the morning." Point!

"I don't have anything to talk about." I won the match! I stomped off to my bedroom with a definitive stride of victory. I had won the verbal and emotional battle—or so I imagined. That night, the muffled sounds of crying could be heard both downstairs and upstairs. The morning sun shone on two pillows soaked with tears—her pillow and mine.

Chapter 24

Cleo

FIFTEEN YEARS OF AGE, I was pregnant, and my hormones and emotions were on a virtual roller-coaster ride! I tried to wish the situation away. That didn't work. Jeremy Edward's sister had told me to drink some turpentine mixed with sugar. I tried to do that, gagged, and then threw the toxic mixture away. Hmmm. I will be like Scarlett O'Hara. I will think about what I will do tomorrow.

My nightly job was to thoroughly clean the kitchen before Mommy left for work at the hospital at 10:00 p.m. The maneuvers were prescribed. Wash the dishes and then pour boiling water over them while they are in the drain basket. Wipe off the stove, behind the stove, the refrigerator, counters, and cabinets. Empty the garbage. Wipe out the garbage can and reline it with fresh newspaper. That kitchen had to be hospital clean when Mommy walked through for a cup of coffee before leaving for work. The night of the flying skillet, Junior had come in after the kitchen was cleaned and proceeded to prepare himself something to eat. Mommy had stopped chastising him for not being home for dinner each night. When he was not there, no dinner was set aside for him. He would have to fend for himself, and that was the source of all the clanking that I heard going on in my just-cleaned kitchen. I saw Junior sitting in a chair with the garbage can about two feet from him. He was peeling potatoes with a potato peeler and attempting to "shoot" the skins into the garbage can. Some of the skins made the can, and the others were on the floor. To add insult to injury, Junior had the big black cast-iron skillet on the stove with the gas flames turned up high. He was frying potatoes, and as he tossed the raw pieces into the skillet, hot Crisco bubbled on the stove top and on the back wall!

"You better have that mess cleaned up before Mommy wakes up!" I yelled at him.

"You shut up, you skunk! You don't tell me what to do! I'll knock your damn head off your neck!"

Junior hauled off and gave me a backhand slap so hard that my head jerked around. That was it! It was on! I punched Junior in his jaw and then proceeded to pick up and throw everything I could get my hands on at him. He turned to run when he saw the knife he had been using to cut potatoes with become a projectile aimed at a live target—him. He made it around the corner of the kitchen into the den as the black cast-iron skillet still bubbling with Crisco shortening and potatoes took flight and crashed through the back window. I followed him with a steam iron, a can of green peas, and a bottle of Del Monte Catsup. He barricaded himself in the bathroom just in the nick of time. One second later, and the can of green peas would have connected with his head. The bottle of catsup hit the wall in the hallway and burst sending streaks of red up and down the hallway. About this time, Mommy emerged from her bedroom, and she shrieked when she saw all that red fluid dripping down the walls.

"Oh my god! They are killing each other!"

The entire drama probably lasted less than two minutes, although it seemed like a lifetime to me and Junior. The neighbor's husband came over as soon as he heard the skillet go through the window. It didn't take long to calm me down. My resolve was, "If he ever puts his hand on me again, I will bash his head open with that skillet!" Junior declared that his sister was crazy and needed to be in the mental hospital.

Junior never hit me again after that night although later he did tyrannize each of his wives and subsequent lady friends. I credit myself with having taught my brother two important lessons that night.

1. Don't tangle with a woman in her kitchen.
2. Don't even think about trying to physically harm a woman who is no longer afraid of you.

CHAPTER 25

Willetta Mae

THE YEAR 1929 WAS A year never to be forgotten. That was the year of the Wall Street Crash and the start of the Great Depression. The St. Valentine's Day Massacre took place that year. The hula-hoop and the yo-yo were invented. Police killed nineteen Mayday protesters in Berlin, and I came into this world born in a hog pen.

During that epic year in Marshall, Texas, a lot of white folks finally realized what being poor meant. Colored folks always knew, but the white folks who felt that they were of a superior class to the colored forcibly learned a new song to sing. Folks who had depended upon farming for their livelihood were disillusioned when the prices for their crops sank so low that they could not make their mortgages nor payments on their farm equipment. Foreclosure, eviction, and repossession became operative metaphors for what was going to happen tomorrow. Once-proud folks had to go on relief, and they were scorned by those who were able to survive without the government handout. The white folks' anger at the government and frustration with their impending poverty brought out the nastiest of nasty in even the ones feigning to be Christians who would sing and pray in church on Sunday morning and be out "coon hunting" the same night. Hateful thoughts toward the colored farmers who appeared to be surviving grew rampantly. The few laboring jobs that were available paid the colored workers less than the white workers, hence, two colored men could earn what would be paid to one white man.

114

White unemployed laborers labeled by their own as "white trash" became stigmatized and threatening to not only the colored but also to the Mexican workers who came across the border and would work for even less than a colored man. White women who had been accustomed to having help to wash their clothes, scrub their floors, and care for their children had to do it themselves. Lynchings were up. Colored farms were burned to the ground. Arrests of colored men who were sentenced to work farms more than quadrupled. Into this hornet's nest of an environment, I, Willetta Mae Rodgers, was born.

My mother's name was Cerena, and I have imagined how I came to be since she never communicated any of the details to me. On the day that I was born, her father and stepmother were getting ready to go over to the Bishop Farm to help with the hog killing. Folks from the church would routinely help each other with the hog killings, going from farm to farm until all the deeds were done. Cerena was glad because she hadn't been feeling too well these last few days. In fact, she had thrown up her breakfast every day for the past month. Her stepmother, whom she called Mama, was real stern with her and would not let an upset stomach hold as an excuse for not getting her work done. She had overheard Mama talking to her Aunt Valeria about her.

"She is a big black girl with nappy hair. The only way she's gonna find herself a husband is if she can work hard right alongside of him, cook good, and keep his house clean."

"She is gonna have to keep him happy in the bedroom too. Even so, he will probably still run after a yaller meriney colored woman— just like what happened with you."

"Aw shush, woman. My husband's first wife was low sick near to dead when he started to court me. My first husband was already dead, and we had no chilluns. I did that woman a favor. I took care of her until she died, and now I am raising her daughter. No, Cerena will need to be really strong and dependable if she is going to find herself a husband around here. The big black not-so-pretty girls be the last ones to get chosen. You know I'm telling the truth."

Cerena had experienced joy when Ubadiah Crayton started to notice her. A good-looking boy, high yellow with wavy hair, and seventeen years of age; she was just thirteen when he convinced her to let him "play with it a little" under the bush arbor at the end of last summer. He held her, told her she was a special kind of pretty and that he loved her. She succumbed to his charms, and they met under that bush arbor the entire month of August. When the summer was over, he enlisted in the Army to help bring needed funds to his family, and he left Marshall. He wrote one letter to her, and then there were no more. His family let everyone know that he had married a high yellow girl from Tyler, and she was going to go with him wherever the Army sent him.

Cerena wondered how he could do such a thing to her! He had professed his love for her, but he must have been lying. It must have been because she was so dark and did not have that pretty hair like the other females in his family.

When the pains began to really hit her with a vengeance, she wanted to die. Grateful that her father and step mother were gone, she had to make plans on what to do with what was about to happen. She had seen countless barn animals give birth, so when the fluid rained down and that mucous plug slid between her thighs and hit the floor, she knew that she didn't have much time. She made it outside to the hog's pen and crawled inside. No one was there to hear her as she cried out in pain during what seemed like hours of labor. She delivered the bloody bundle right there in the hog's muck. She lay there relieved of the hours of torturous pain and did not move until the after birth made its way out of the birth canal, slipping and sliding into the hogs' muck where she covered it and the infant as quickly as she could. She was thinking that the infant would die and the hogs would eat it up. No one would ever know that she had given birth that day.

Her father and stepmother finally returned home before nightfall because it just was not safe to be colored and out on the open road after dark. Her stepmother came right into the house while her daddy put the horse in the barn. Within minutes, he came running up to the house to get his wife. He had heard some strange sound coming from the hog pen. He grabbed his shotgun and with Mama made it to the hog pen in time to rescue the infant who was about to be chawed by one of the largest of the hogs.

Cerena was sent away to live with her maternal grandmother. Her father and stepmother told everyone at church that Cerena was needed in Longview to help the grandmother who was ailing. Everyone suspected the truth but did not say anything. Her father and stepmother kept the baby with them on the farm and raised her until she was ten years old. The baby, me, lived a good life on the farm where I was cherished by my grandparents. After all, I was born with a yellow complexion and wavy hair, just like my biological father.

Cerena's maternal grandmother eventually passed on to glory, and Cerena married a service man and moved to California. She never had any more children, and she devoted her life to her husband, Mozelle Sanger, who was as black complexioned as she was. He swore that he loved her in spite of her dark complexion! Things progressed well for Mr. and Mrs. Sanger. They worked side by side—he in the shipyard and she in the canneries. They saved their money and invested in real estate. By the time I came to live with them, they owned a home and several apartment buildings in the city of Berkeley, California.

My grandfather had died, and my step-grandmother, Mama, was low sick with the big C. She could not continue to care for me, so she reluctantly sent me to live with my birth mother. I had cried and begged Mama to please not send me away. I had promised Mama that I would take care of her while she was sick, but I was packed up and sent to California to be with my birth mother, Cerena. Mama died shortly after I arrived in Berkeley, California.

My mother, Cerena, did not appear to be so happy that I was finally living with her, but her husband was overjoyed. Mother had not seen me since the day I was born, so she had no idea how pretty I was. I was a mellow yellow in color, and I had long wavy hair. I was a big girl, like she herself had been, only I was stacked like a brick outhouse! Mother had been a big girl at that age, but she had been big and boxy. They say it looked like I was already sixteen years old. Mother did not like the way that Mozelle looked at me. He would carefully watch me while I was eating, and he would carefully watch me while I completed my chores. It was as if he was studying me.

Mother began to hit me for any infraction that she could think of. I didn't fold the sheets correctly. *Whap!* A slap across the face. I was caught mopping the kitchen floor with a mop instead of being down on my hands and knees with a cleaning rag. *Whap!* A slap across the face. Mother claimed that I was wiggling my behind when I walked in front of Mozelle. *Whap!* A slap across the face. I did not make the beds correctly. *Whap!* A slap across the face. I was slapped across the face daily for a variety of offenses. The greatest offenses being the way I looked and the fact that I was there. To make matters worse, Mozelle had started to pay peculiar attention to me, whom he nicknamed Willie Mae. Always watching me, he would see me go into the bathroom, wait just long enough until he was sure I was sitting on the commode with my underpants down, and then he would walk in on me, stuttering in nervousness.

"Oh, excuse me, Willie Mae. I ... I ... I didn't know you was in here" was his constant excuse. He would do the same thing when I took my baths. He would wait long enough for me to be naked and in the bathtub when he would rush in there stuttering.

"I am sorry, Willie Mae, but ... but ... but I can't hold it."

Then he would stand right next to the bathtub, expose himself, and urinate into the commode all the time carefully watching me to see my reaction. When I would complain to my mother, she would call me a liar.

"What do you think he wants with your big ole fat ass? You yaller curly-headed heifers think that every man wants you, and it ain't so!"

"Mother, can I put a lock on the bathroom door so he can't come in on me?"

"No! Locks on bathroom doors are dangerous. Suppose you fall or get sick? No one can come in to help you if the door is locked. No, you just stop displaying yourself to Mozelle. He don't want you, you hear me? He said that you be coming in on him when he is in there, and I want that to stop right now. Do you hear me!"

By the age of sixteen, I was married to a Navy man, living in my own apartment with my own husband, and looking forward to the birth of my first child. I was out of that hellhole that my mother,

Cerena, and stepfather, Mozelle, resided in. My first child was a boy, and I named him Clark. Four years later, my second child, a daughter I named Ranethia was born. I told Mother and that Mozelle point-blank that if he ever put his hands on my daughter the way that he tried to put his hands on me, I would see him dead and buried in the ground before the sun set on his mangy ass. Mother slapped me in the face for being so disrespectful to her husband, but this time, I didn't give a damn!

CHAPTER 26

Willetta Mae

At the age of thirty-five, I had remarried to a man six years my junior named Marvin. At first glance, Marvin seemed to be an all-right sort of guy. He worked for the General Motors Plant in Fremont, played baseball for recreation, rode a Harley Davidson motorcycle, loved to play cards, and he loved to barbecue goats. I already had my own home when I met Marvin, yet in a moment of blind passion, I agreed to place his name on the title to the property when we married. I was even planning to have a child with him. Not long after the first year of wedded bliss, the real Marvin started to come out. He faithfully went to work five days a week. He would also faithfully play baseball, ride his motorcycle, and drink every weekend. If he made it home, he made it home drunk and was completely unaware when I went through his pockets and removed money. Sometimes, he was so drunk that he did not even make it home.

Marvin was in agreement with Cleo entering the family domicile as a foster child, and he was in agreement when I spoke to him about bringing her infant son to live there as well. Within six months, he stated that he wanted to get some foster boys who were old enough for him to teach to play ball and take fishing, so I contacted the Foster Care Agency and arranged to open the home to two young males, Leroy (aged thirteen) and Raymond (aged eleven). Marvin took them fishing one time, claimed they made too much noise while on the boat, and never took them again. He never took them to the ball park, and he never wanted to participate with them in the role of a father. He treated them as if they were unwelcome boarders.

Raymond was a loving child, but he was hardheaded. The night the gun went off, Raymond had been painting his model cars in the garage-turned-bedroom and in the hall bathroom. There was model car paint all over the bathroom sink, the walls, and on the door. I was not feeling well, so I implored Marvin to discipline the boy. I was tired of being the only one talking to him.

"I'm not gonna say nothing to him. I don't care what happens to him. Send his ass back to San Francisco for all I care!"

"That's why we don't want to call you Daddy! You don't act like one!"

I couldn't believe that retort came out of Cleo's mouth. Marvin looked at her in utter disbelief, and then he swung his fist toward her head muttering, "Ain't no chile gonna disrespect me in my house!"

Cleo saw his fist coming and ducked just in time. His fist instead of connecting with her head, just grazed the top of the pink plastic curlers she had just rolled her hair up with. Four of the rollers cracked and fell to the floor. Seeing this, I jumped up directly in front of Marvin and yelled, "I told you to never put your hands on one of these girls!"

He slapped me across my face so hard that I fell back against the wall for just a short period. I regained my balance and quickly headed for our bedroom with Marvin in hot pursuit behind me. He knew that he had blown it, and he knew what I told him I would do to him if he ever put his hands on one of the girls or me. Everyone in the house could hear me rummaging around under the bed for the gun case, and he was trying in vain to curtail me. I saw Cleo grab her son out of his crib, and she had made it out of the den door when the gun went off. Marvin took off running as Cleo sprinted three doors down to a neighbor's home, where she called for police intervention. She and Baby Jonathon remained with the neighbor until the police arrived, and then they came back to the home.

Marvin came back to the house when he saw the police vehicle. Yes, he was alive and well, and he was insisting that I be arrested for discharging a gun at him. I was calling him a blatant bald-faced liar. The police searched for the gun and could not find it. Marvin insisted that I had fired a bullet at him, and it must be somewhere in the bedroom. The police searched and searched. They found neither a gun, a bullet casing, nor a fired bullet. They suggested that Marvin leave the home that night and perhaps come back the next day when everyone had calmed down.

That night, Ranethia (my daughter) and Cleo retrieved the gun from the neighbor's backyard where it had been cautiously thrown into the fishpond along with the shell casing. We searched the bedroom for the discharged bullet, and we found it wedged in the wall behind the drapery rod of the bedroom window. The angle suggested that I was on the floor of the bedroom firing upwards. The bullet had missed Marvin, and he had hightailed it out of there when I discharged it.

The next morning, after breakfast, I preached to the girls, "Always keep your own money. Don't be so dependent upon a man that you cannot exist if he favors you not to. If you buy your own home, never put a man's name on it. If he wants a home, he needs to buy himself one. Never let a man put his hands on your girls. Men are too strong, and they will hurt a girl. *Never let a man beat on you.* If he does it once, he will do it again. Never go up against a man with just your hands. He is stronger than you, and you will need an equalizer. The best equalizer is a gun because you can shoot him before he gets up on you. And if you take out a gun on him, be prepared to kill him with it. A knife he may take away from you and use on you. Let him know that if he tries to come into the ring against you, with hurting you on his mind, he may whoop you once, but he will leave that ring with some lifetime scars *if* he lives to tell about it."

CHAPTER 27

Willetta Mae

EVENTUALLY, I PUT MARVIN OUT of the home. His weekend dalliances turned into week-long absences. The woman he was sleeping with had taken to calling me late at night and playing music like "The Thrill Is Gone" to me over the telephone. She once had the nerve to call and tell me that when she was through with me, she would have my house, my car, and my man! To add insult to injury, I could stand on my backyard patio, look over the fence and down the hill to observe Marvin's truck parked in front of her residence! Marvin tried repeatedly to dismantle the Dodge Monaco that he had given to me for a birthday present, claiming that his new woman needed it. He also threatened to legally take the house away from me.

One night, I grew emotionally tired of the games that Marvin and his woman were playing. The woman had interrupted my soaking bath with the latest irritating telephone call. That woman had told me that she was going to do something so that the next time I got into that car, I would not be able to get out of it. "I ought to come up there and just whip your ass!" she had drunkenly threatened. "Well, you had better bring your lunch with you because you will be here all damn day!" I had retorted before I slammed down the telephone. I started to make plans then on how to rid myself of the menace of that woman and of Marvin, my former beloved. Around two in the morning, I, along with Raymond and Leon, had driven down to the woman's residence and sliced all four of the tires on

123

Marvin's vehicle. We would have gotten away unseen and unheard if Raymond had not started stuttering, "M-M-Mama, sh-sh-should I c-c-c-cut the other car tires too?" The lights in the residence went on, the window was opened, and we were observed leaving the scene of the carnage.

We had borrowed Miss Josephine's car for our tour of duty that night, and we had just parked it in her garage and made it into the house when the police and Marvin came flying down the street. The boys hopped into bed with their shoes on, and I went to bed also. It took several minutes for the front door to be opened to the police knocks, and when it was opened, Marvin stormed into the living room with two police officers demanding that I be taken into custody immediately. I appeared in my nightgown and peignoir, curlers in my hair, slippers on my feet, and I feigned complete ignorance of what Marvin was yelling about. I told the officers that I and the children had been in bed asleep when the loud knocking occurred at the front door. The officers peeked in on the boys, and they seemed to be asleep. They checked the hood of my Dodge Monaco, and it was cold. It had not been recently driven. I told the police officers that, yes, I was aware of where my husband was spending some of his evenings and with who. I told them to look at the house that this girlfriend was renting and compare it to mine. There was no comparison. His lady friend did not have anything that I wanted, and in fact, I wished them well. Marvin and I were going through a divorce, and he was angry and wanted to get back at me because I had told his lady friend about two of his other "women." He and the lady friend tended to get drunk and harass me! All I wanted was peace so that I could continue to raise the children that had been placed in my care. The police told Marvin that there was no evidence that anyone from that home had been involved in the mischief that took place with his automobile. They advised him to go home, and they apologized to me. They left.

An hour after the police had left, they were summoned back again. In retaliation for him calling the police to my home, I had piled all of Marvin's articles of clothing into a pile on the cement patio in the backyard, soaked it with lighter fluid, and lit a match to it. The bonfire could be seen all the way to where Marvin and his lady friend were still fuming over the destruction of the tires to the vehicle parked in front of the residence. Someone had called them on the telephone and played the song "Hit the road, Jack, and don't you come back no more, no more, no more, no more." I doused the flames as requested by the police, and everyone went back to bed. No charges were made, nor were there any arrests that night.

I may not have had a formal education, but I was much smarter than Marvin could have ever thought to even pretend to be. I filed for divorce, and in my request for settlement, I asked for spousal support for two years because I had miscarried Marvin's child and needed time to get back on my feet, and I asked for child support for Cleo's son, whom I claimed that Marvin and I had adopted. Marvin did not have enough sense to know that the so-called adoption papers he had signed but did not have notarized were worthless pieces of paper. He did not hire an attorney to represent him, and the court ruled in my favor ordering spousal and child support along with the sale and split proceeds of the family residence in two years. Marvin did not pay one red cent toward the spousal support nor toward the child support. When I went back to court at the appointed time, I had evidence that Marvin had not complied with the court orders. I asked that his name be taken off the title to the family home, and in exchange, he was relieved of the responsibility of paying back spousal support and child support. This request was ordered by the court.

CHAPTER 28

Cleo

RAYMOND WAS THE TYPE OF child who could endear emotional feelings on both sides of the parental continuum. He was as black as tar, skinny, and his right eye had been nearly destroyed when his brother hit him in the head with a toy truck when he was around five years of age. Raymond looked like a humanized version of Atomic Ant—you know, long skinny neck, peanut head, and eyeglasses. On the positive end, Raymond was such a loving entity. He would bend over backwards to make you happy, was comical, could put together anything, and he was so sincere. On the negative end, Raymond was a ten-year-old disaster. He would stutter when trying to avoid telling the truth, refused to eat fresh vegetables, preferring sugar water, potato salad, Hostess CupCakes, and baked beans. He refused to bathe and brush his teeth until threatened, and he kept the most incredible pile of junk under his bed. His under-the-bed treasure chest included old bicycle parts, pieces of model cars, baseball equipment, Hostess CupCake wrappers, popsicle sticks, empty Big Gulp cups, and cardboard—any type of cardboard box that he had retrieved from any garbage can on the block. He used to always say that he was going to make something out of it. What he made was a pile of junk that would scare the disease out of a swamp rat. It was that pile of junk that earned him the most whoopings from Aunt Willetta, our foster mother.

Raymond and Leon had come to Aunt Willetta's home as foster children at the insistence of Aunt Willetta's husband, Marvin.

Marvin had claimed that he wanted some boys that he could teach to fish and play baseball—activities that he never involved himself in. Ranethia and I played baseball with them, had rock fights with them, rode bicycles with them, took them to the movies and football games—in short, we did the things that Marvin did not do, and we loved them dearly.

Aunt Willetta had turned her two-car garage into a large bedroom. She had the walls covered with sheetrock, painted, and a ceiling light installed. She had the garage door removed and a large picture window and a small entrance door installed. The final touch was the linoleum floor. This room was the room for the boys with the household entrance a door that separated their room from my bedroom. The only non-bedroom entities in this space were the water heater and a chest-style deep freezer.

Ranethia and I would go shopping at the commissary with my military dependent ID card, and we were able to pick up great bargains: bicycles, milk, bread, meat, laundry products, ice cream by the ten-gallon container, and bags of cookies that had to be at least three feet tall. The edible items were all placed in that chest-style deep freezer so that there would always be enough when needed. The strangest things would always happen to those cookie bags. Within weeks, one bag would completely disappear while the other bag would be nearly empty with only a smattering of crumbs in the bottom of the bag. Aunt Willetta would ask each of the seven foster children as well as her daughter, Ranethia, if they had touched those bags of cookies. Every child answered, "No," except for Raymond. He would start stuttering as he explained what he thought happened to those thirty-six-inch-tall bags of cookies.

"I … I … I am not saying that Leon did it, but … but … but I kind of did … did … did see him st-st-st-standing by the freezer one day … day … day with his h-h-h-hand on top of it."

Aunt Willetta would look under Raymond's bed and find an empty cookie bag hiding amongst the other prized relics that he kept stored there. She would pull back the covers on Raymond's bed, and there would be the telltale sprinkling of cookie crumbs between the sheets and a few remaining cookies stuffed inside his pillow case.

"That's it, I am gonna whoop your behind!" and she would head to her bedroom to retrieve a weapon of butt destruction suitable for the task of whooping Raymond. Raymond would make a beeline under his bed, and you could hear him rummaging for his lone instrument of salvation, a small Gideon's Bible that he always kept there for important praying sessions.

The scenario unfolded like this: Aunt Willetta, a 240-pound ball of Texas born, caramel-colored anger dressed in a pink housecoat would come charging into the boys' room wielding that belt and verbally chastising Raymond. Raymond would be on his knees, one hand on the Gideon's Bible and the other hand trying to grab the offending weapon out of her hand, and Pepi, the dog, barking furiously while trying to nip at Aunt Willetta's ankles. Raymond would appear to be in deep prayer, kneeling toward the east as fervently as a member of the Muslim religious sect. His prayers were intersected with his pleas to Aunt Willetta for forbearance.

"One more chance."

"Our Father who art in heaven, please sp-sp-sp-spare me on this day."

"Mama, Mama, Mama, p-p-please, just one more chance."

"Mary Mother of God, p-p-p-please save me."

"Oh, Mama, Mama, Mama, p-p-p-please, I p-p-p-promise I won't do it anymore."

"I'm gonna change! I'm gonna change! God, have mercy! I'm gonna change."

The welts on Raymond's arms and legs would raise up before she even finished. The last twenty blows with that belt were dealt with the following syllabic promise,

"Every ... time ... you ... do ... this ... I'm ... gonna ... whip ... your ... be ... hind! Do ... you ... under ... stand ... me? Huh? Do ... you? Huh?"

Before she retreated to her bedroom, Aunt Willetta had popped Pepi upside the head with the belt for having the audacity to act like what a pet dog is, a protector of children. She whacked each one of us who had been watching the melee and laughing at the comedy show. She directed me and Ranethia to pick up her favorite Chinese food and ordered Raymond to clean up his face, clean up the crumbs, and clean up that mess under his bed. Raymond would put that Gideon's Bible away as quickly as he had pulled it out, take off his bed sheets and shake them out in the backyard before making his bed up again, and he would move some of the junk under his bed from one side to another.

Raymond's whoopings usually took place on Friday nights. Since there was no school the next day, we would all retire to the living room to watch *Creature Features*, eat hot dogs and BBQ, baked beans, or pizza for dinner, and fall asleep on the floor, which prompted Aunt Willetta to pop us all with that same belt amidst our pleas of, "I wasn't really asleep. I was just resting my eyes."

So much has happened since Raymond was that ten-year-old boy getting his butt whooped nearly every other Friday. Ranethia and I went off to separate colleges. Leon's girlfriend became pregnant, and Aunt Willetta made sure that he married and promised to stay with his wife and child. Velma joined the United States Army. Josephine married, but the frustrations of not being able to conceive a child with her husband led her into a life of alcoholism. Mitzi became a flower child at the age of twenty-eight. She passed away at the age of fifty, and no one seems to know the details. Jordan became a professional dancer, proudly professed to a gay lifestyle, and made a life for himself in Las Vegas. Sheila became a mother at the age of nineteen, and without the help of a father, she raised a spectacular son who has made a career of the United States Air Force. She is now a proud mother-in-law and grandmother. Jonathon married, and has been the most fantastic father of three children (all grown and college educated). Raymond developed diabetes, suffered with it for a number of years before succumbing to it.

I think about Aunt Willetta, who passed away in 1997, and the children she opened her home to. She was a kind and loving woman. I remember the words the pastor spoke during her funeral: "All you foster children had family members somewhere who did not want to be bothered with you. She took you in, gave you a bed, a pillow, and a blanket. She made sure you were fed and clothed, and she did it when someone else in your family could have, but no one else would."

As children, we formed a tight alliance. United we stood because we had no intention of falling—not as long as we had each other. Ranethia and I intervened in situations with the younger ones that might have resulted in neighborhood fights. We tutored them with their studies, and I even wrote a college history paper for Raymond one time because he just could not get it together. I helped Ranethia to write not only the commencement speech for her high school graduation but for her college graduation as well. I also wrote the winning essay for a scholarship that was awarded to Velma. Broken hearts were massaged in that house. Disappointments were trivialized in that house. The love and support surrounded the perimeter of that house. Nothing and no one outside of that house could hurt any of us who lived together in that house.

The memories of that house located on Grant Street in Vallejo are thought-provoking and sweet. Sweet because of the affection, protection, and nourishment we provided for each other. Thought-provoking because the type of punishment that Raymond endured every other week remind me that so many of us still believe that a good sound beating is the only way to modify a child's behavior patterns.

Chapter 29

Cleo

THAT BOY WAS GOING TO have to learn his lesson, and he would have to learn it good. I felt as if the eyes of the world were upon me, judging my movements to determine if I was good enough to call myself a "mother." Aunt Willetta, my foster mother, had preached long and relentlessly to me about not being a "sorry mother." I had to be a good mother, put my child first, and ensure that he had everything he needed in life despite not having a father around.

Aunt Willetta often retold the story of how she had singlehandedly raised her son by herself and had made a man out of him. The task did not come without challenges like the time she had to beat him when he was sixteen and had the gall to tell her what he was not going to do. He had wanted to go to a party, but she needed him to stay home with Ranethia, his younger sister, while she went to work as a hostess at a nightclub. He told her he was not the babysitter, and he was going to the party. She had leapt upon him like a tiger, ripping his new red mohair sweater from his back and leaving bleeding claw marks from her long fingernails when she slapped him several times across his face. He had run from the home, and he decided to turn his mother in for child abuse. She was nearly ready to leave for work when the call came from the police department.

"Ma'am, your son is here with bloody scratches on his face that he said you gave to him."

"I did."

"Well, ma'am, you should consider other ways of disciplining your son other than beating him like that. You can be arrested—"

"Hold it! He is my son, and I am his mother. If he doesn't mind me, he won't mind anyone, and that includes you. I beat his behind for being insolent, and I know that if you stop him on the street and he is insolent with you, a beating is the least that you will do to him. You will shoot him! Am I not right?"

"No, hold on there, ma'am, we don't go around shooting kids—"

"You a damned lie! Now you look a here, I am going to raise my son, and if I have to kill him to make him do right, I will do it. I will do it before I let you gun him down in the streets like a damn dog!"

"Ma'am, he is here at police headquarters, and we have no reason to keep him here. He has not broken any laws yet. Can you come and get him?"

"Ask him how he got down there."

"How did you get down here, son?"

She could hear her son grunting a response in the background.

"Ma'am, he said that he walked down here."

"Tell him to walk his behind back home and to do it now because I cannot be late for work."

Her son made it back home in record time. He walked through the front door and went straight into his bedroom. His mother went to work.

This was the role model that I had before me. It did not help that this same foster mother constantly threatened to "keep that chile myself before I lets you ruin him." I was admonished daily with, "You ain't gonna be able to raise that boy. He gonna whoop your behind before he turns seventeen. You going to have the same problems out of him that your momma had out of your brother. He better be glad that she is his mother and not me, because I don't play! I'd have that butthole crawling up the walls using his eyebrows for leverage if he ever tried to talk to me like he talks to her."

All this was catapulting across my psyche like ping-pong balls as I prepared to punish my nine-year-old son for destroying an antique Meerschaum pipe left to him by his late godfather and then lying about it. The foster mother was going to whip him, but she decided that his natural mother needed to do it.

"Whip his behind real good so that he understands that you are the boss. If not, he will soon be whipping you!"

I had to show her that I had control of the situation, so I started to beat my son with an extension cord, the weapon of choice to teach a hardheaded boy child a lesson he would never forget. I actually channeled myself into the body and mind-set of the foster mother so that I could demonstrate that I could do a good job of disciplining my own son. Oh my god! When I was done, my son had bleeding welts on his forearms and legs! I couldn't believe that I had done that and left the bedroom torture chamber in tears. The foster mother offered comfort by telling me that I hadn't done anything wrong. He deserved the whipping, and this was only the first of many to come if I was going to be successful raising him by myself.

"A little bit of bleeding ain't gonna kill him. When the police beat him, they will do so with rubber hoses that will only leave bruises. That is if they don't shoot him down in the streets like a dog. You done right."

I took him home with me and attempted to follow the usual routine of dinner, television, bath, and then bedtime. Unable to sleep, I quietly left the apartment and drove to a nearby telephone booth to call my then fiancé who lived in another state. I wept into the phone as I told him of what I had done, expecting him to also tell me that it was all right. He did not.

"Baby, you drew blood? You are not supposed to beat a child until he bleeds, I don't care what Aunt Willetta says. It ain't right. You were wrong! Don't whip him again. I will be there in a couple of months for good, and I will take over the discipline. It takes a man to raise a boy to become a man, and you have demonstrated that you cannot do it by yourself."

That was the first statement made by any man in reference to the incorrect method of disciplining a black male child. The second statement I overheard the next day while shopping with my son. We had passed through the pharmaceutical area of Walgreens when I turned back to pick up some cotton balls. I overheard two white male clerks having a conversation behind the counter.

"It's a damn shame when someone beats up on a kid like that! She ought to be in jail! Did you see those marks on his arms?"

Those words cut like knives into my heart because I knew they were talking about me, and they were right. A black woman had told me to beat the hell out of my son. A black man and two white men stated that such punishment was wrong. I knew they were right. This was the beginning of my break from some of Aunt Willetta's teachings. I would be strong, and I would raise my son, and I vowed never to hurt my child like that again nor let anyone else.

CHAPTER 30

Cleo

I HAD FIRST MET KINGSTON because of Phillip. Phillip had been my buddy since college days. The two of us would go to parties and nightclubs together, separate, keep an eye on each other, and serve a rescue mission when it looked like someone undesirable was trying to make unwanted conversation. Phillip would give me the eye when a female he did not want to talk to got in his face. I would saunter over to where Phillip was, put my hand on his shoulder, and tell him that it was time to dance. He would do the same for me—more times than I needed to save him. We had a very good system and a very good friendship. I could talk to him about anything, and he shared a lot of male scheming wisdom with me so that I would know what to look out for. He didn't like the fact that I had started to keep company with George, who was separated from his wife, and so he orchestrated an introduction to Kingston. He had told me that there was a barbecue party that he wanted to go to, and I had agreed to go with him. When we got to the apartment complex, there was no party, and Kingston was the only person home. Phillip found some excuse to leave, and Kingston and I were there to get to know each other. Kingston apologized for the lack of a barbecue party, but he asked if I would at least stay for dinner. I agreed, and the rest is history.

He wrote me poetry that he would mail to me from whatever location IBM had him working from, and he worked all over the state of California. When he was home, he took me out to dinner, and before we left the restaurant, he would order an additional take-out dinner complete with salad and dessert for my son to enjoy at home. He told me of how he knew what it felt like to grow up without a father in the home. His had died when he was two years old. The series of lovers that his mother had were inconsequential and only contributed milk, shoes, and perhaps a light bill here and there. He had vowed that if he dated a woman with a son, he would treat him as if he was his own son. For Christmas, he supplied a new ten-speed bicycle, weight training equipment, and other things that males enjoy. He had a daughter, and I was inquisitive as to why he had not married the mother. He told me that he loved and was supporting his daughter but that he could not fathom a life with the mother. He said that she was crazy and that her mother and grandmother had advised her to conceive this child due to the type of professional job that he had with IBM. In essence, he felt that he had been tricked. She had told him that she was practicing birth control, and she was not.

When the call came, I talked with her. At first, she would not give her name—just the request to "tell your man to stay away from my house." Eventually, she identified herself, and we spent quite a bit of time conversing about Kingston, their daughter, and his mother. My curiosity got the best of me, and I went to visit the woman on my own. She lived in a Section 8 housing unit not far from Kingston's mother. She answered the door at 1:00 p.m. still in pajamas with pink sponge rollers in her hair. She was very hospitable and clucked on about how happy she was to meet me. Since she was the mother of his only child, she had to get to know his fiancée because we would be in communication with each other regarding the child. I learned that the woman had only completed high school, had no ambitions, and yes, her mother and grandmother had told her to "trap" Kingston. If she gave birth to the only child of an only child, his mother would make sure that this child was taken care of, and since IBM did not lay off employees (at that time), he was assured of a good-paying job for the rest of his life.

She claimed that Kingston was coming to her in the wee hours of the morning to have sex with her, and she was tired of it. When

I left her apartment, I felt sort of relieved. I did not believe that Kingston was in any way still interested in her. If he went there at all, it was to see his daughter, and he had confirmed that he only saw her when she was visiting with his mother because it was less hassle than dealing directly with her. I could understand why Kingston would not have chosen this woman for his wife. If I had been a man, I would not have chosen her either. One difference between his actions and mine is that I would never have (as an adult) taken up enough time with her to conceive a child. There was something odd about this woman, and I determined that she was emotionally unstable—might have been a special needs student while in school. In any event, she had reached the top pillar of where she was able to take herself, and that was on the top rung of Aid to Families with Dependent Children. She had an apartment, food stamps, and a child support check that came every two weeks. There were things that I could do to assist the little girl, and I resolved that I would do these things. Kingston and I continued to make our wedding plans.

The day I walked down the aisle to marry Kingston, I was a happy bride. My best friend from college, my sister, and foster sisters were my attendants. Kingston's daughter and Ranethia's daughter were my two flower girls. My oldest brother gave me away. While I was taking that march down the aisle, I was thinking to myself, *If it doesn't work, I can always become single again. I am going through the front door to this marriage, but there is a backdoor if I need it.* When the minister asked, "If there is anyone here who objects to this marriage, let him speak now," there was a mild chuckling when Kingston made a complete 180 degree turn to scan the audience to see if there was someone there with "something to object to." Seeing no one, he returned to his place, exchanged vows with me, and we were pronounced man and wife.

The reception was wonderful! I was so excited that I nearly forgot to eat. The photographs, the well wishes, the hugs, the gifts! When we finally made it up to the honeymoon suite of the hotel, lo and behold, the room was spiderwebbed with toilet paper! We ate a little of the supper that some kind soul had packaged and sent upstairs. Probably the same kind souls who had webbed the suite with the toilet paper. We drank champagne, opened a few gifts, and then he asked me if I would like to try some "snow."

"Snow, what is that?" He produced a small light blue foil package that I had seen a man hand to him at the elevator. I initially thought that it was a condom as a joke. But, no. The package contained powdered cocaine, and he was asking me to try it!

"Hell no! You know I don't do drugs. You need to flush it down the toilet."

"No, he paid for this. I will just give it back to him when I see him and let him know that me and Baby Girl don't roll that way. Don't worry about it."

The rest of the evening was absolute bliss.

CHAPTER 31

Cleo

THE MARRIAGE TOOK PLACE ON the first weekend in October. On Halloween night, Kingston did not come home. A drunk man had banged on the front door, demanding to be let in for the party, not believing me when I told him through the door that there was no party there. That drunk man yanked open the garage door and commenced to bang on the door to the kitchen, and that is when I called the police. They came and arrested the man. I fumed while I cleaned the kitchen. I had a husband, a six-foot, two-inch husband, and I had to call the police to protect me from a crazy drunk man at home. I began to think about that backdoor.

Right after the Christmas holidays, the baby mama dropped her four-year-old daughter and a large box of clothes on the front doorstep. I suppose this action was intended to cause friction in the marriage, but it did not. I fell in love with LaJuana and began to treat her as if she was my own child. I took her everywhere I went, to shop, to exercise class, to bowling, and to visit my friends who had small children the same age. I told Kingston that he needed to start the proceedings to get full custody, and he balked. He balked when I found a Discoveryland Preschool less than two blocks from the school where I was employed.

"I can drop her off on my way to school and pick her up on my way back home."

"No. There is no need to spend that kind of money. I don't go to work until 3:00 p.m. She can stay here with me, and Jonathon can watch her until you come home."

"No. Jonathon [my fourteen-year-old son] does not need to be responsible for a child. He is not old enough. Besides that, he would have to give up his afterschool sports. If money is your major issue, then you keep her here in the morning, and then you can take her to Discoveryland Preschool. We will only be charged for the time that she is there, a half day at the most."

"No. I will take her to my auntie, and she will watch her for free until you get off work."

I did not really want LaJuana to spend that kind of daily time with the auntie. That particular auntie was almost a replica of the baby mama, just an older version—AFDC, food stamps, sitting around the Section 8 housing unit all day in a bathrobe. But I decided not to fight him. LaJuana was his daughter. The only time I bucked was when he wanted to buy some used bedroom furniture from one of his coke-headed friends. I said, "No." We would get her new furniture, to which he said, "No." Consequently, we didn't procure any furniture, and LaJuana slept on the pull-out sofa bed in the living room.

Having his daughter living under the roof with him did not change his weekend routine. I was so disgusted with him on the Friday night when I had taken LaJuana with me to the bowling alley for a tournament. She had a ball playing with the other children. When we left, the car just stopped at a red light two blocks from the bowling alley. She and I walked to a phone booth to call home. He was not there. I left a message on the answering machine, letting him know where we were and what had happened so that he could come to get us. He never did. After waiting for two hours, we walked back to the phone booth and called for a taxicab. I left the car in the middle of the street and took LaJuana home. He had not made it home yet. Early the next morning, he still was not there. I asked a neighbor to take me back to where the car might still have been. This neighbor knew a little something about cars, and he was able to get the car started, and he followed me back home for safety. It was about

6:30 a.m. when we pulled up. Lo and behold, Kingston was pulling up at the same time. I didn't want to look at him much less speak to him. I was stranded at night in East San Jose with his daughter, and he was out pilfering somewhere all night long. Backdoor, where in the hell are you?

The baby mama had started calling to check up on her daughter. I would gladly converse with her and let the child talk with her. If Kingston answered the telephone, he would rudely hang up on her. She called me one day at work crying and told me that she had just called the house to speak with her daughter, and he had told her the child was dead! I began to pressure him to take legal action, and he refused to do it. When the county sheriff called to talk with me, he told me that he understood the emotions behind the situation, but the mother had legal custody. Kingston would have to either petition the courts for legal custody or give the child back to her mother. I tried to reason with Kingston that evening when he came home, but he would not agree to seek legal custody.

"I don't need no court to tell me that she is my daughter. I have rights, and I don't have to pay no attorney to exercise them. No! I am not going to seek custody. I already have custody!"

The next day, the sheriff called me again. He told me that if the child was not returned to her mother immediately, he would go to Kingston's place of employment and arrest him on the spot. It was up to him. I told the sheriff to let the baby mama know that she could come and pick up her daughter.

She came within twenty minutes to pick up her daughter, and with tears in her eyes, she thanked me profusely for helping her. I called Kingston at work and told him what had taken place and why I had given LaJuana to her mother. He pretended to be angry with me, but it was short-lived. His attitude and actions told me that he was actually relieved.

The movie *The Color Purple* was released in 1985, and boy did it cause a stir! Some black folks were complaining that it depicted black men in a negative light. Others complained that it pointed out the weakness in a black woman. Another opinion was that there were not enough positive black movies available at the theaters, and this one was just so negative. My opinions were not popular at all, and many times my opinions stirred the nest during a brunch or after movie discussion. I let it be known that I actually felt sorry for Mister, the character played by Danny Glover. He was not able to marry and live with the one woman he truly loved, and in the end, that woman and his common law wife became closer than he ever could have imagined. He was left to walk his land with his old broken-down horse all alone. Sophia was a character who had my admiration, and four years after my divorce from Kingston, I could relate to statements she had made as well as a statement that was made about her.

Mister had told Harpo that "Sophia thinks too much of herself ... needs to be taken down a peg or two."

Kingston's friends (the fellas) had nicknamed me Miss After-Five and Miss Supper Club. When I inquired what this meant, Kingston said that it meant that I thought that I was too good to take a drink of liquor before five in the afternoon, and I would only go out to a fancy supper club—never a hole in the wall to eat dinner.

"Okay," I said. "That would be correct."

He then told me that the fellas claimed that I thought too much of myself and needed to be slapped upside the head.

"I told them that me and Baby Girl don't roll that way. If I have to beat my woman, I am going to leave her," he stated in a braggartly way.

Kingston referred to the members of my sorority as Kappa Sappas, women who were hoity-toity.

"You married one, so you must be inclined to the hoity-toity type," I teased him.

"All you women do is get dressed up in that sickening pink and green, go to tea parties, and then talk about each other's husbands like they are dogs."

"Well, if it looks like a dog, smells like a dog, and wags its tail like a dog, it is probably a dog. If you don't want to be classified as a dog, don't hang out with dogs, and don't bark like one."

My grandmother had told me that all men had at least one cup of dog meat in their recipe, and some of them received more than one cup issued. Kingston had begun to display his dog tendencies shortly after the wedding. He would not come home on Friday nights. Sometimes, his overnight excursions were two days or more. He started off with lame excuses of being drunk and falling asleep in the car and the fellas would not let him drive home because he had consumed too much alcohol. And one time he even concocted a story about being arrested for falling asleep in the car while parked in a red zone. To make matters more discerning, his baby mama would call me about ten minutes before he would pull up to let me know that he had just left her apartment. I never could convince her to call me while he was there, not after he left. I told her that I had no intention of hurting her. I just wanted to see him come through her door with my own eyes.

"Oh no," she would say. "If I do that, he will stomp my ass into the ground."

"Why do you let him come in at all if he treats you like that?"

"I guess that I just love him in spite of it. I don't know how to get away from him."

"Easy, just put one foot in front of the other and keep on stepping if that is what you really want to do."

The arguments over this disgusting and disrespectful behavior continued, and eventually, I insisted that he leave. He refused. I started packing his belongings in the fashion of the Native American women of the Eastern Woodlands tribes that I was teaching my eighth graders about. When the woman of the longhouse wanted to be rid of the husband because of his lack of performing husband responsibilities, she simply packed his belongings and placed them outside of the residence. That was the Algonquin, Cayuga, Onondaga, Oneida, Seneca, and Mohawk way of divorce. As Kingston's transgressions grew, the location of his belongings moved from the closet in the spare bedroom to the front porch to the front sidewalk. The night that my next-door neighbors decided to move was consequential. Kingston had not come home for two nights, and it was Sunday evening when he marched into the house as if he was about to go to war. I was in the kitchen, preparing a vegetable salad for a sorority function the next day. I had a radish carving tool in my right hand. Kingston stomped into the kitchen and loudly demanded that I go outside and bring all his things back into the house. The fellas had driven by and seen his belongings on the curb, and they had laughed at him. "Hey, man. Looks like you have been put out … again!"

When I refused to comply with his demand, he physically dragged me outside to the front yard and proceeded to tear my clothes from me. He had already ripped the sweatshirt that I was wearing, and when he tried to pull it over my head, he received a cut on his cheek from the radish carving tool that was still in my hand. When he realized that he was bleeding and that the offending tool was still in my hand, he backed off me. He threw his belongings into his car and sped off down the street. Hmm. I guess his momma never told him that it was a bad idea to attempt to fight a woman when she was in her domain—the kitchen.

I called his mother the next morning to tell her what had happened. What did I expect? She was his mother, not mine. She never asked me if he hurt me or if he had hurt my son.

"Is he going to have a scar in his face?" was all that she could muster.

"Probably. But if he ever puts his hands on me again, he won't have a scarred face. He will have a lifeless body."

"Well, if anything ever happens to my son, all I want from you is his body so that I can bury it as I see fit. I don't want to have to come through you for nuthin'!"

"You don't have to wait until he is dead to come and get his body. You can have it now while it is still drinking and acting a fool. Just know that if he puts his hands on me again, that body will come to you in a pine box!"

I thought of that conversation when in *The Color Purple* movie, I heard Miss Sophia tell Miss Celie, "I loves Harpo. God knows I do. But I will kill him dead before I lets him beat me."

His mother had been a source of interruption and deceitful actions from the beginning. She had told Kingston that I must have been a woman "kept" by older mens, and that was how I was able to buy two houses on my own. Those older mens helped me. She made it a practice to come by my home when I was not there to visit him so that she could rummage through kitchen cabinets, bathroom cabinets, and bedroom closets. Whenever Kingston and I were having issues and he had temporarily moved in with one of the fellas, she would show up at my house with the baby mama in the car to ask where her son was staying. I was hip to her. I was not going to disrespect and argue with her, but I was not going to allow her to dictate what went on in my home either. She had once told me that she hated the Baby Mama and used to pray to God that she would just die so that she could raise that grandbaby herself. I had nicknamed her the Black Widow because of her evilness. There was no doubt in my mind that she had no affections for me even though I was married to her only child.

Kingston usually tried to make amends after we had argued. He would bring flowers, come in and mop floors, wash my car, and pick up our favorite take-out dinner when he was trying to say that he was sorry. This time, he came over and told me point-blank that he was tired of trying to get along with me. He ought to just take his half of the two properties and go on his merry way. That is what the fellas told him that they would do in the same situation.

"And I suppose that one of those numb nut fools has convinced you that you have some degree of ownership in something that you did not buy? Some idiot without a pot to pee in or a window to throw it out of is telling you that you have vested interests in my home and my rental property."

"I have been here paying bills on this house. I bought a new water heater, and I put new screens on all these windows."

"And you had a place to live during this time. If you live somewhere, you have rent to pay. If you eat, you must buy groceries. If you shower, you must pay for water and soap. Go ahead and listen to the experts who have so much real estate coming out of their ears that they don't know their asses from a hole in the ground. All you are going to do is generate more costs for each of us in legal fees. You think that I am as stupid as your fellas. You should know better by now."

I was furious with him for even making that statement. When we married, we had agreed to live on one paycheck and save the other so that we could purchase our own home together. We would sell my home to get the down payment, and we had agreed that if anything happened to the marriage, the proceeds from the sale of my home would not be considered community property. That amount would be returned to me and the balance of the assets be split up. When we met with a realtor to talk about this venture, Kingston turned tail on me. He sat like a stone statue in the meeting, not having much to say at all. When we got home, he told me that he did not want to buy a new home with me.

"The mortgage notes are going to be around $1,200 a month. That means $2,400 the following month if we miss a payment."

"Miss a payment! Why in the hell would two grown-assed Negroes working full-time miss a payment? You just do not miss a mortgage payment ever!"

Then I thought about his mother and her habit of getting two and three months behind on her car payment. The car would be repossessed, and she would be trying to borrow from every Tom, Dick, and Kingston to get it back. His mother had never owned property and probably didn't have the vaguest idea of what it took to even qualify for a mortgage loan. She had once told me that any man coming around her had to bring something, and she kept three or four of them for different financial needs while her son was growing up. This one helped with the light bill, this one bought milk and cereal, this one bought her son's shoes, and that one helped her to buy his shirts and pants. I could understand his reluctance to tie himself down with a mortgage. He was not used to such money management. Our plan to save one of our checks and live off the other did not work, and we closed the joint account. I paid my house note, and he paid the utility bills. We both bought groceries, and we individually took care of our own vehicles. The only time he brought up home ownership again was to insist that I put his name on my home. He claimed that he ran the streets on the weekend because he did not have a home of his own to come home to. Backdoor, where are you?

By June, I had already prepared the divorce papers, and they were on hand to be filed when he committed another outrageous act of disrespect. That opportunity came on the Juneteenth weekend. I had complained so about his nocturnal absences that he promised to stay at home that Friday night. He was so nervous and jumpy. He was as fidgety as I supposed an alcoholic or a dope addict might be going "cold turkey." He was argumentative and demanding. He demanded that I prepare him a full-fledged meal at 11:00 p.m. because he was "hungry." He tossed and turned all night and tore out of there like a bat flying out of hell the next morning. He didn't return until around 7:00 p.m., and one of the fellas was with him. He went straight to the bedroom, and I heard the shower. I noticed that this fella was dressed in a suit and tie, so I asked him where he was off to. He said that he and Kingston were on their way to a dance. I went into the bedroom where Kingston was getting all dressed up to go out.

"Am I not invited to go to this dance with you?"

"The invitation only said Kingston. Your name wasn't on it. You are not invited."

"I'd like to go too." And I went into the bathroom to get my makeup kit.

"You ain't going no place with me. You are fat and ugly, and I am embarrassed to be seen in public with you."

He then snatched my makeup kit and threw it out of the patio door. He threw it so hard, it went over the fence into the neighbor's yard.

"And if you leave this house tonight, I am going to stomp your fat ass into the floor," he threatened.

"Kingston, if *you* leave this house tonight, *you* are never to come back. I have the divorce papers already filled out, and I will have *you* served tonight. It will be *over*."

He and his fella left and went to the dance. True to my threat, I got on the telephone to find someone who would serve him the divorce papers. I started with the husbands of friends. None of them wanted to be involved in my domestic situation. I drove out to his favorite watering hole located near the freeway, located his car in the parking lot, placed a copy of the papers on the steering wheel, busted the bottle of his favorite whiskey on the sidewalk, and then I went back to my car. I decided that I had better do this the right way and really have him served. The first man that I saw drive up was approached. I asked him if he would serve the papers. He declined. The second man that I saw drive up was approached. I asked him if he would serve the papers. He also declined. The third man that I saw drive up was approached. I had twenty-five dollars cash in my hand when I asked him, and he agreed.

Kingston came storming into the house around 5:00 a.m. and immediately assaulted me. He picked me up out of the bed and threw me across the room into the wall.

"Where are my wedding rings!" he demanded. "You want to leave me, you can't take my wedding rings with you. You are not going to be lying up in bed with some other man, waving your legs all up in the air with my rings on your finger. I will kill you first!"

He grabbed for me as I ran past him to get to the car. He nearly tore my nightgown off! When I made it outside, I locked the double-sided dead bolt in the front door with the key to give myself more time. It was just enough time for me to get into my car, turn on the engine, and start to back away before he came tearing out of the house after me.

"Open this damn door!"

When he realized that the car was in motion, he hauled off and struck the windshield with his bare fist not once but twice. The entire front windshield cracked from the blows, and I continued to back the car out of the driveway. Once on the street, I had to lean my head out of the driver's window in order to see where I was going because the entire windshield was shattered.

The first stop I made was Amy's house. She did not answer her door. I then went to a telephone booth about a mile away. She didn't answer her telephone either, so I called the police and explained what had happened. I was advised to wait there in my car. An officer would arrive soon. Forty-five minutes passed, no officer. I called again. I was told to be patient. There was a shift change coming up soon, and an officer would be dispatched. Another hour passed. During that time, I reflected on my life and the mistake I had made marrying Kingston. Then I reflected on the fact that I was sitting outside in a car nearly naked with a torn nightgown and no shoes while he was probably snoring in my bed—my warm bed!

I reflected on the life that my son and I had before Kingston. We were just fine! Aunt Willetta's son and daughter-in-law had cosigned the mortgage loan for the first townhouse that I had purchased. Jonathon and I supplemented the grocery budget by picking wild mustard greens in the field across the road after a good rain, and we put them in bread bags and froze them storing the bags in the upright freezer that Aunt Willetta had given to me. When the television was broken and I could not yet replace it, Jonathon and I had frequented libraries and bookstores. We read prolifically and discussed the books that we had chosen. I remember choosing the book *Roots* at one of the bookstores. It had not become a bestseller yet. I chose it because it was thick and by an author that I admired. I assumed that it would give me days of reading pleasure. I sold that townhouse to a friend and her husband to get the down payment for the current home, and every cent that was earned from the sale of the townhouse went into the down payment. When I purchased the current ranch-style home, Mommy had loaned me the money I needed to clear out all my installment debt. Mortgage lenders did not like to see credit card balances when approving a mortgage loan. Jonathon and I earned grocery money that summer delivering the San Jose Mercury, the Evergreen Times, and fliers from Newberry's Store. We bought eggs from the egg ranch and milk from the dairy because the items cost less there. When we went to the drive-in movie, we took our own snacks of burritos, popcorn, grapes, and lemonade to save money. We budgeted, and we made it.

Now, that drunk, coke-headed son of a bitch was lying up in my house that he did not help pay for, had tried to destroy my car that he did not pay for, had physically assaulted me, and I was out here in the cold, nearly naked! My anger almost turned to nausea, and I at this point seriously contemplated taking his life. Ooh, if only I had a gun! I could march back in there and blow his drunken and coke-fogged head off! In fact, that is exactly what I decided I would do! I called Amy's number again because I knew that she had a .38 revolver. She still did not answer. The next call I made was to Diedre, who lived in Fremont. Diedre answered the phone, listened to my story, and told me to come on up and get the gun. She would wait for me. The last call that I made from that phone was to Aunt Willetta's number. She rarely answered the phone that early in the morning, and I was banking on Raymond answering it. He did.

"Raymond! I want you to very quietly get dressed, get in the car, come to San Jose and get Jonathon. Take him back to Oakland with you and keep him with you for the weekend. Can you do that?"

"Yes. You want me to drive to San Jose to your house and get Jonathon, bring him back up here with me and keep him for the weekend, right? What's wrong?"

"Kingston jumped on me this morning because I had him served with divorce papers. I am going to a friend's house to get a gun, and I am going to blow his ass out of there!"

"No, you don't! You just stay right there. I am on my way!"

Aunt Willetta had picked up the extension, and she had heard everything.

"Do you hear what I say? You just stay right there until the police come. We will come and get Jonathon."

The telephone disengaged, and within twenty seconds, it was ringing. This time, it was the police who informed me that an officer was on his way. Two officers arrived within five minutes, and they followed me back to my house. They asked me to wait outside while they went inside to talk to my husband. After about fifteen minutes, they came back outside.

"Ma'am, I don't see any bruises on you. Did the glass cut you or anything?"

"No. You don't see any bruises on me because it is too early. He threw me into a wall early this morning. I ran to get away from him."

"Ma'am, he said that he did not touch you. He only hit the windshield of the car."

"Can you see the damage he inflicted on this car? I must hang my head out of the side window in order to drive. He is crazy, and he is probably all tanked up on some narcotic. Please get him out of the house. My son is in there."

"Your son is all right. We saw him sleeping in his bedroom. Ma'am, there is no law against a man breaking the windshield of his wife's car on private property. If you are not hurt and we see no evidence that you are, no crime has been committed here."

"Well, I have a carload full of folks on their way here from Oakland. If you don't get him out of my house, I guarantee you that they will!"

The vision of angry black people coming down from Oakland must have popped a kernel in the officer's reasoning process.

"From Oakland, you say?"

"From East Oakland!"

"What did you say his name was again? I think that I did see a bench warrant for someone with that name. We will take care of it."

The two officers went back into the house, and within two minutes, they reappeared with Kingston handcuffed. After they put him into the patrol car, they advised me to get my son and consider sleeping somewhere else that night. They would only be able to hold him for about four hours.

"Thank you, Officer."

That patrol car must have passed Aunt Willetta's station wagon on the road because she pulled up within five minutes of their departure.

"Where is the son of a bitch?" she asked as she stepped out of her vehicle.

She had brought Raymond, Leroy, Uncle Jeff, and Jackie with her. She meant business. She understood that the police had taken him away, but she decided she was going to stay there and wait for him to come back. She directed her crew to help me pack up Kingston's things—everything, including the floor-model television his mother had given us for Christmas last year. Once it was all packed, it was driven to the home of one of his friends that I had called. While all this packing and moving was going on, Aunt Willetta took a seat on the living room sofa. She had a loaded .38 revolver that she put on her lap and then covered with a throw pillow.

"When he comes through that door, I have just one question to ask him. Why did you put your hands on her? If he gives me the wrong answer, and he will, I am going to blow his mangy ass away!"

I went into the bedroom and called the police department to ask how long Kingston would be detained. They told me that he would only be detained for up to eight hours, and then he would be released—probably between four and five that afternoon. They suggested that I take my son and spend the night somewhere else until I could get a restraining order to keep him away from the property. I thanked the officer and told Aunt Willetta that he would not be released until the next day. She would not need to stay all day. I had made reservations for me and Jonathon at a hotel downtown. We would be all right. Jonathon had summer school starting the next morning, and I had a summer school class to teach as well.

I loved Aunt Willetta. She had been a safe port in the troubled storm for me when I was in a very perilous state. Becoming a mother at the tender age of fifteen was traumatic. Leaving my own mother's home at the same age was traumatic. I was considering placing my child up for adoption because I didn't want him to live under the influence of Junior, and I had no way of taking care of him by myself. I had learned that his biological father was a lying, indecent, and irresponsible person who had fathered numerous children. My son was the first of three babies born to high-school-aged girls in just that year. There were more to follow. I had run away from home once before, and then I came to Aunt Willetta. She had told me that I did not need to run anymore because I could live with her. Her only requirements were that I obey her and get an education so that I could take care of my son in the way that he should be taken care of.

When I first ran away to her home, she took me down to my mother's home and told Mommy in front of me that I could stay with her as long as I minded her. The first time I did not mind her, she was going to beat my ass. The second time I did not mind her, she was going to bring me back. Aunt Willetta convinced me that I should not place my child up for adoption. There was no guarantee that the adoptive family would love and care for him as much as I could. She had survived a tumultuous upbringing herself, and she was determined to help any child (particularly a female child) who came her way needing help, and that is exactly what she did.

To make a long story short, I dearly loved Aunt Willetta, and I did not want someone I loved to be in danger of having to serve time in jail because I had made a bad decision in choosing marriage to someone as unfit for marriage as Kingston. I wanted to protect her, so I made her believe that Kingston would be locked up for twenty-four hours so that she would go back home. She believed me. After she was assured that I did indeed have the reservation for the hotel, we all left my house together. Jonathon and I went to the hotel while Aunt Willetta and her entourage went back to Oakland.

A tragedy had been averted. Had I followed through on my plan to annihilate Kingston, I could have lost everything I had worked so hard for. My college degrees would be useless, my educational service credentials would probably be revoked, the home that I was so proud of would probably need to be sold to pay for legal fees, I would spend time in jail (perhaps a woman's prison), and my son would have to grow up bearing the shame of a mother and biological father who had stepped above the law. I never wanted my son to be in the position that Junior was in—having to lie in bed and pretend to be asleep while his mother was being beaten in the next room. I never wanted my son to feel that he had to take action against an assaultive stepfather and, in doing so, place his own safety in jeopardy. I made the correct decision that day. I sent Aunt Willetta home so that she would not betray her own well-being while defending mine. Before the year was ended, that backdoor that I had envisioned during my wedding ceremony opened, served its purpose, and was shut by the court forever.

CHAPTER 32

I Remember Vonellen

MY BEST FRIEND WAS TURNING fifty. Her sisters and I wanted to make it special, so we arranged for one of her childhood friends from Louisiana to be there as a surprise. The friend's name was Vonellen, and she was quite a character. After the party guests had gone home, the three of us sat up all night just talking. After a while, it was just the two of them talking and reminiscing about growing up in the Ninth Ward of New Orleans.

"I never told you this, but when we were in the third grade, I used to wish that I was you."

"Why?"

"Because you always seemed like you had everything you wanted, that's why. I wanted to be you just to see how it felt to be loved by everybody."

"Vonellen, you got to be crazy. I wasn't loved no more than you were."

"Yes, you were."

"No, I wasn't. I got my butt whipped for coming home late from school, just like you. Your daddy's mother lived in the house right behind you, didn't she? My daddy's mother lived in Mississippi. My father's sisters didn't like my mother, so we very rarely went there. Why you say that?"

"Remember how you used to wonder why I never invited you over to my house to play? I always wanted to come over to yours?"

"Yes. I thought that you didn't want me to come to your house for some reason. Maybe you thought it was too far for me to walk."

"Naw, that ain't why."

"Why then?"

"First of all, I didn't want you to see where I lived. You and your sister and brothers had a nice house with three bedrooms, a kitchen, and a living room. All we had was one bed in a bedroom that we slept in and a small kitchen. When you walked in the front door, you walked into our bedroom. If you walked in the backdoor, you walked into our kitchen. The bathroom was a closet just off the kitchen—and I do mean a closet—a toilet, a sink, and a narrow shower. Whenever you came home from school, Bobbi was always there in the kitchen getting supper started while your mama was at work. Ooh, I remember the smells coming from that kitchen. Every time we went to your house after school, I could count on some good smells—chicken frying, greens cooking, cornbread baking, and some sweet potatoes. There was always something. If you said you were hungry, Bobbi would either make you a peanut-butter sandwich, give you a piece of cornbread with butter and honey, or give you a chicken wing. She and your mother treated me just like family. They would give me whatever they gave you. If Gussie was at home when I got there after school, there were never any good smells like that. Most of the time, Gussie wouldn't even be there. One time, I remember I tried to play like I was you when I came home from school. I bounced into the room and tried to tell Gussie all about what had happened at school that day, then I asked for something to eat. Gussie told me to go and fix myself an egg."

"Girl, I didn't know that. All that time I thought that you were so cool. You didn't let anything or anybody bother you. I remember you used to always say, 'I don't care,' and snap away from anyone, young or old, who got on your nerves. I wanted to be just like you."

"And I wanted to be just like you. Bobbi used to do your hair, and it was always so pretty. I liked the way she curled your bangs. I could always tell when your father was home and tried to comb your hair for school. The part was always a little crooked. Some of the kids used to laugh at you behind your back, but I used to wish that I had a daddy who would care enough about me to help me get ready for school. I stopped letting Gussie comb my hair when I was eight. She used to hurt me, jerking my head every which a way and burning me when she pressed it."

"Girl, I think that all of us used to hate getting our hair pressed. It took so long, and if you moved, you did get burned or popped with a brush for having a rubber neck. Ha ha ha. My mother used to get so impatient with me and my hair. She would press my hair, and within two hours, it was nappy again. We could never understand why. Mommy thought that I was running around outside playing, and sometimes I was, but most times I wasn't. It just used to nap up so quickly. She would run a warm comb through it every night before I went to bed so that Daddy would be able to comb it the next day. It was not until I was forty-three years old that I realized that I had an ongoing thyroid problem that caused me to sweat profusely."

"There were times when I couldn't come into the house after school if Dukes was there."

"Who in the hell was Dukes?"

"Gussie's old man, if that's what you want to call it. I knew when he was going to be there because Gussie would tell me to not come home straight after school. On those days, I usually came home with you, or else I went home with Marvalene. I didn't like going to Marvalene's house as much as yours because her folks wouldn't invite me to eat with them. I would sit in Marvalene's room until they had all finished eating. If there was anything left, her mother would invite me to 'have some.' I always politely said, 'No thank you.' Soon, I would head for home. The day I walked in on Gussie and Dukes was a day that I just did not want to stay in Marvalene's room through their supper. I told everyone that Gussie was fixing us something special for supper and that I had to go home. When I got home, the TV was on, but the lights were out. I figured that Gussie had fallen asleep with the TV on, so I opened the door. Damn!"

"What do you mean *damn?*"

"Just what I said. Damn! Gussie was lying up top of the bed, buck bald with her legs spread apart—toes trying to reach for the ceiling. Dukes was on his knees, pounding his big thick black hairy thang into her private thing. His scrotum looked how I imagined gorilla balls would look—big clumps of walnuts stuffed into a pair of black water balloons, and they were banging against the tips of her butt cheeks. And it smelled to high hell in there!"

"Girl, you mean they was doing it? Right there on your bed?"

"Right there on my bed. They didn't even see me, so I closed the door and crept around to the backdoor. I let myself in the kitchen and sat quietly while they finished. That bed was squeaking on its springs, the headboard was bumping against the wall, and Dukes was just slobbering. 'Mine! Mine! Yeah! Yeah, baby! Right like that! All this here is mine! Ain't it? Ain't it? Tell me it's all mine, baby! Make it talk! Make it walk! I'm gonna whoop me up some nooky tonight! Give it to me, baby! Oh yeah, baby! Baby, you got it! You got it! You got it!'

"The bumping became more rhythmical and fiercer with each succeeding jab of his thang. I seemed as though he might knock the headboard through the wall. I sat there alone in that cold kitchen, wondering how it would feel for a man to sweat, cuss, and while standing on his knees, violently pound his thang into my thang with his balls whooping my butt in concert. Would it hurt? Would it feel good? I screamed at the same time that Gussie screamed—a sharp painful howl that wound down to a moan. At least, I thought I screamed. I thought that Dukes had killed her, so I ran into the room where they were and turned on the light. They were a slimy and sweaty mess, my bed a mess, and the room smelled even worse that it had the first time I walked in on them. I never could understand how people could pay to go to pornographic films. Seeing someone else in a sex act is just about the grossest thing you ever could want to see. It is just plain nasty!"

"Oh my god! That was something for an eight-year-old child to see. Did you ever tell your mother that you caught Gussie doing it in y'all's bedroom?"

"Hummph, girl. Gussie was my mother."

CHAPTER 33

Vonellen

EVEN THOUGH VONELLEN WAS THE childhood friend of my best friend, I continued to keep in touch with her after the surprise birthday party. She was so witty and naturally entertaining. Her name was always a source of intrigue, and I once asked her what it meant.

"My name is actually a combination of my paternal and maternal grandmother's names. One was named Yvonne, and the other was named Hellen. You will find a lot of combinations like that coming out of Alabama, at least that is what I think. I know of girl babies named Vontrese (Yvonne and Theresa), Vonchelle (Yvonne and Michelle), VonMelody (Yvonne and Melody), and me, Vonellen (Yvonne and Hellen). Don't ask me why the name Yvonne was incorporated like that. I am sure there is historical significance, but I just don't know what it is."

Vonellen died last year. She complained of a severe headache while at the gym one afternoon. She passed out right there on the treadmill. They rushed her to the hospital, but she expired before they arrived. She was gone before she had a chance to mingle with the members of her high school class during their upcoming fortieth reunion. I recalled a time she called me at three o'clock in the morning Pacific Standard Time. I thought the woman had lost her mind.

"Girl, ooh yeah. Girl, oh girl, oh girl!"

"Vonellen, girl what is wrong with you. Have you been drinking?"

"Lawd, have mercy no. No, not tonight. Ohhhhhhhhhhhhh hhhhhh!"

"Well then, what is wrong with you? Why are you talking like you are sick? Are you sick? Did you fall? Have you been taking your medication?"

"Oh, Lawd! Oh, Lawd! Oh, Lawd! It's Terrence! Oh! Oh! Ohhhhhhhhhhhhhhh! Hooooooooooey! Girl, girl, girl, girl, girl!"

"Vonellen, was he in an accident? Did something happen? What is going on? Can you talk to me? I can't understand what you're trying to tell me. Stop crying and tell me what's happened. Can you talk?"

"Talk? Girl, have you ever tried to talk on the phone while the rim of your jelly jar is being licked?"

In the background, I heard a man's pleading voice say, "Baby, you not supposed to be on the telephone, telling it!"

Click.

Vonellen was not physically abused by her mother, but she was subjected to what I consider to be extreme psychological abuse. I am not sure which mode of abuse is the least destructive. Vonellen did not have a warm and loving home as a child, nor did she have a warm and loving relationship with her mother. She was not taught how to love and respect, and as a result, she grew up into an adult who just did not care about the feelings of others. She had bragged to us about meeting up with some of her high school friends every year in New Orleans. Most of them routinely came home during August for the homecoming programs at their parents' church, so this group of five had made arrangements to meet during this time each year for an afternoon of lunch and shopping. Vonellen went each year, but she only went to lunch. She told them that she could not take off the time from her job that had her working weekends. In reality, she had lunch with the girls, and while they were out shopping, she was engaging in a sexual rendezvous at the Holiday Inn with one of their husbands. They did this every year until Vonellen's departure from this life.

CHAPTER 34

Cleo

I WAS IN CHURCH SERVICE one Sunday, minding my own business and really getting into an enjoyable mode of worship when a deaconess sitting behind me reached under my hat and pulled at the hair on my nape.

"Girl, you need to do something with that kitchen! Looks like BB shots!"

Now, a younger and less-sophisticated Cleo would have answered her with an insulting retort, possibly criticizing the lop-sided worn-out wig that was sitting on top of her head, but I chose to publish my remarks on my Facebook page instead.

> My kitchen, nape, is considered "rough" by some of my sisters. It has been described as naps, BB shots, balls, you name it. I don't get offended because I used to refer to my kitchen in the same way. Thank God that I am proud of my natural hair and how it looks. My BB shots relate directly to the fact that I have chosen not to burn my hair out with chemical overprocessing or pressing, not to rub it out with consistent wearing of wigs, and not to pull it out from the roots with weaves and tight braids. My BB shots are reflective of my hair's healthy condition—the hair that

God gave me, the hair that I love. Every woman demonstrates her love for herself in unique ways, and I am not here to judge anyone. By the same, don't judge me because I choose not to care for my hair in the same way that you care for yours—whether it is yours by growth or yours by purchase. Love ya!

CHAPTER 35

Ms. Ida

Ms. IDA, AS MY MATERNAL grandmother was called, was a small woman not to be taken lightly. Mommy and Aunt Ginny used to always talk about how their mom used to whip them when they were kids. They were whipped when they did not work fast enough in the tobacco fields. Working fast enough meant that they kept up with Pop and their brothers Calvin and Harvey. They were whipped for having the nerve to sass her, which Aunt Ginny routinely did. They were whipped when they did not get home on time. This little petite 105-pound, five-foot-one-inch-tall Attila the Hun was a force to be feared.

Mommy often told the story of how she and Ginny had gone to get their hair pressed by Mrs. Jenkins. Mrs. Jenkins lived several miles from home, but she would press the girls' hair in exchange for jars of Grandma's homemade marmalade or quarts of her homemade grape wine. One of the days when the girls had appointments for the hair pressing, it started to rain, and Mr. Jenkins would not let them walk home. He told them that when the rain let up, he would take them home in the wagon himself. Mommy and Aunt Ginny tried to tell him that they had to wrap their heads up real well and get home because Mom wouldn't accept any excuse for being late. Mr. Jenkins would not hear of it, and the girls had to stay there until the rain let up several hours later. True to his word, he took the girls home in his wagon. When he got there, he explained to Ms. Ida that the girls wanted to walk home, but he prevented them from doing it. He didn't want them walking in that weather all by themselves. Ms. Ida thanked him and asked him to have a bite of supper before he left. Mr. Jenkins had some cold fried chicken, sliced tomatoes topped with vinegar and black pepper, cornbread, and coffee before he went on his way. He hadn't even turned onto the road before Ms. Ida turned on her daughters with vengeance. She whipped them until their legs and arms were bleeding. She didn't care what Mr. Jenkins said; she had told them what time to return, and they had not obeyed her. That merited a whipping, and they readily received one. The next day, she would not let them wear long sleeves to hide the scars of what had taken place. She wanted everyone at church to see. Folks at church saw the welts and said nothing. Whippings were personal matters between the family members. It was no one else's business.

Another whipping story that Mommy and Aunt Ginny used to tell was about the time that Aunt Ginny was tied up in a tree with a fire lit under her. That story was hard to believe, and I was sure that Mommy and Aunt Ginny had enhanced the facts to make the story more excitable. Apparently, Grandma was tired of whipping Aunt Ginny because that stubborn girl would place her hands on her hips and not cry—not matter how hard and long she was whipped. To show her who was really the boss, Grandma had hung her in a tree by her hands and built a fire on the ground around her feet. When Ginny started to feel the heat of the flames on her feet and legs, she hollered. She hollered and bellowed so loud that folks from the neighboring farm came to see what was wrong. Seeing Aunt Ginny hanging in that tree by her hands with a live fire at her feet, the neighbor went to get Grandpa, who came quickly on his horse.

"Ida Elizabeth, cut that girl down!"

They say that Grandma tried to explain why she was doing what she was doing. "You don't know what this girl has done to me ..."

Grandpa bellowed, "I said cut that girl down and do it *now*."

She quickly put the flames out that had started to sear the soles of Aunt Ginny's shoes, and then she cut the rope that held her up by her hands. Grandpa put Ginny on his horse and took her back to the house. Now, I did not believe that story.

I went to visit my maternal grandma the year that I turned twenty-four. I took my son with me so that he could experience Dr. Greenwood at least once. Dr. Greenwood was the nickname that Grandma gave to the dogwood tree switches that she would use to spank us when we were children. We usually got spanked for not following her directions—like going down to the creek when she told us not to. She and Grandpa warned that moccasins and quicksand were down at that creek, so Junior and I went down there daily trying to find what they described as danger. We had the ultimate plan. We walked in the water one ahead of the other. That way, if the one in front got caught in the quicksand, the other one would pull the victim out. Needless to say, we never saw any moccasins, and we never found the quicksand. What we found were the switches that Grandma made us get when we returned. If we didn't get a substantial switch, she would go out and bring back a branch. So we learned to get decent switches for her to employ with our butt whippings. The butt whippings obviously were not that bad because we dared to break her rules and go down to the creek each and every Saturday after breakfast and chores were over, knowing that a butt whipping was coming when we got back home. The excitement of looking for moccasins and quicksand was worth the few minutes of switching that was coming. Now, at age twenty-four, I smiled when Grandma admonished my son and told him to stay away from the creek because the moccasins and quicksand were down there.

"Grandma," I said, "there were no moccasins and quicksand down there. Me and Junior looked high and low for both the Indian burial ground and the quicksand. We never found either. You and Grandpa were just trying to scare us, weren't you?"

"Indian burial ground? I never said nothing to you about no Indian burial ground! I was talking to you about the water snakes. They were called cottonmouth moccasins, and they are poisonous! That's right! I whipped y'all's tails every time you went down to that creek because you could have been killed. Y'all were some hard-headed kids. I whipped your tails for going to the outhouse when it was night-time because rattlesnakes like to curl up in there at night."

I almost fell out of my chair. "What? Poisonous snakes?"

"That is right. No parent or grandparent enjoys whipping the children, but when they don't listen to you, you have to do something to make them listen. Not listening can cost them their lives."

Now that the door was open, I felt at ease asking her about the whipping stories that I had heard about. I asked her why she whipped Mommy and Aunt Ginny so much.

"You would have to understand what the south was like then. My family was free issue, so we always worked our own land. We worked hard too. Ginny and your mother didn't like to work in the fields. They would lag behind and play games. They would hide and try to smoke. Yes, I tore their tails up every time they did that. The message I wanted them to get was that field work in some white man's field or housework in some white woman's kitchen was all they would have available to them if they did not get themselves an education. When I told them to work hard in the fields alongside their father and brothers, I meant just that so that they would understand what hard work was all about.

"It was also a time when colored children walking at night could be taken by someone. The woods were no place for anyone's child to be when it got dark. When a child was due home at a certain time and did not appear, the worry began. That child could be hanging in a tree somewhere, floating in a river somewhere, or lying up somewhere raped, stabbed, shot, or burned. When something like that happened, and it did happen, there was nothing that the family could do except bury the child. When I told my children to be home at a certain time, I meant just that. We didn't have telephones then, so there was no way to call. All they could do was come home when they were supposed to. When they did not, I whipped them real good."

I told my Grandma that I had overheard Mommy and Aunt Ginny talking about a time when Aunt Ginny was tied up in a tree. I never believed that story. Grandma looked at me and told me that the story was true. She said that Ginny was a stubborn child who would break her rules, sass her, and not cry when she whipped her.

"Aurora was the pretty one. I knew that her worry would be related to a man. As long as she wanted to remain with that man, she could. I would never go into a man's house because of how he was treating my daughter. The first time he hit her would be all on him—the fault, that is. The second and subsequent times that he hit her would be on her as well—her fault for still being up in there with him. She always knew that she could come home, and we would protect her and her children from any harm. Now if her husband come onto my property and try to hurt her, he will surely know something. Ginny was not as pretty as Aurora, so I was not worried about her with a man. She would probably be the one to beat on the man. I was always so worried about that girl. In fact, I was genuinely afraid that something terrible would happen to her because of her mouth and her attitude. A girl who will sass her own mother like that will sass Miss Sally (nickname for any white woman). To sass Miss Sally could mean a severe beating, hanging, burning, and death. I was trying to break her will in an effort to save her life. The day that I tied her up in that tree, I was at my wit's end. She was already larger than me. I was chastising her for not completing her chores, and she put her hands on her hips, rolled her eyes at me, and said 'So?' I had slapped her in her face, and she did not cry. I had whipped her with a belt, and she did not cry. When I raised the cane to her, she threatened to hit me back! I had to do something, so I tied her tail up in the tree and lit a fire under her. You better believe that she started to cry then!"

CHAPTER 36

Strength of Character

SATURDAYS WERE THE ULTIMATE DAYS of joy in my mother's house when *he* was not there. There was always someone there, getting fitted for a dress, getting ready to go make groceries at the commissary, getting their hair straightened, swapping opinions about the "stories," cleaning and picking greens, snapping string beans, canning peaches, making plum jelly, and sharing gossip. Sitting under the kitchen table playing jacks and "listening," we learned the value of a dollar, the value of the black women's barter system, the power of collective work, and the invariable lessons in life learned from either episodes of *As the World Turns* or the current events taking place right in our own neighborhoods. We also learned how to depend upon strength of character when it appeared that everything and everyone was going against you.

These women who came to my mother's house on Saturdays were black women—not wealthy women but women who worked and planned and collaborated and managed to turn lemons into lemonade, vinegar into sweet pickle juice, and salt into sugar. So you think that you cannot turn salt into sugar? Try to sprinkle a little salt on a tart lemon or a fresh slice of watermelon. You will find that the salt brings out the sweetness just as the salt of life brought out the sweetness in these women who were caring for their families on a shoestring yet maintained the strength and dignity in the face of daily assaults upon their ethnicity and gender that only black women can understand.

Mommy was a professional seamstress during her early years. She supplemented the Air Force allowance that Duarté sent her by creating masterpieces that could be seen each Sunday during the Second Baptist Church services. She made the brocade suits and covered high heels and handbags to match. She made the wool suits with fur cuffs and collars. She made the coordinating hats to match. She made coats. She made peignoirs and bathrobes. She made bridal gowns and headpieces. She made the bridesmaids' dresses as well as the flower girl dresses. She made the children's angel costumes for the Christmas play. Easter Sunday could have been her own private fashion show, for her creations were present throughout the church, dotting the assembly hall like a myriad of colorful tulips that all came up at once in a field after a good rain. The lady choir members could not wait to come down from the stands, remove their robes, and join in with the annual Easter parade of finery. Miss Maggie was the lady who could not always pay for her dresses to be made, so she bartered with Mommy for the services. She would straighten Mommy's hair and help her with the canning of the peaches. We, their collective daughters, would play quietly on the floor and listen to their conversations. Sometimes, we were playing so quietly, the women forgot that we were there, listening and learning.

When their conversations began with "Humph, you know she knew better," we girls had to discern if they were talking about a soap-opera character or someone real that they both knew. When they noticed us listening, and we were ignored; they were talking about one of the soap-opera divas. If they made us leave the room or go outside to play, they were talking about a real person who probably went to our church.

The topic of their conversation on one particular day was Brother Fred, his wife, Mother Bea, and Brother Fred's lady friend Miss Dottie Louise. Fred had left Mother Bea for Miss Dottie Louise about ten years earlier. No one could understand why. The two women looked like they were sisters. They each weighed in at over 360 pounds. They each were about five feet three inches in height, and each one was well known for burning in the kitchen. They both loved Brother Fred, but he felt the need to leave one for the other. He had bought Miss Dottie Louise a house, a car, furniture, and he lived with her and her daughter in a family-style arrangement. Now to be fair to Brother Fred, he did try to take care of both households. Both houses were free of a mortgage. He would go into the country every so often and come back with bags of beans, peas, nuts, and potatoes. He would also procure crates of okra, tomatoes, apples, peaches, pears—whatever was in season. He would let Miss Dottie Louise take what she wanted off the top. Then he would let his other lady friends take what they wanted. He always brought the remaining items to Mother Bea and just left them on the front porch. Sometimes, the stuff that he left on the porch was worse than what the county would give to the families that were on relief. But Mother Bea accepted the packages, threw out what was spoiled, and cooked the rest for herself and Halleylou.

Now, the reason for this story: Fred was living with Miss Dottie Louise, but he had never divorced Mother Bea, oh, and he had just died. Mommy was with Mother Bea at the funeral home when she was attempting to make the final arrangements. It was traditional for the spouse to wash the dearly departed's body and dress him for the wake. In the midst of the sponge bathing of Brother Fred, Miss Dottie Louise pushed her way in and insisted that she should be the one to wash his body and make the final arrangements. Mother Bea just looked at her for what seemed like an eternity before saying, "This is a fambly affair, and you ain't part of our fambly."

Miss Dottie Louise was livid, and she insisted that she and her daughter deserved to ride in the funeral car.

"Not in this lifetime," Mother Bea imparted to her.

Miss Dottie Louise turned on her heel and stormed out of the mortuary, mumbling something about how she would get her own car. Well, Miss Dottie Louise learned that not only did Mother Bea have the ultimate right to determine what was going to take place with Fred's remains, but Mother Bea had captured all of Fred's assets, including the title to the house that Miss Dottie Louise was still living in!

The funeral services were only three days away, and the two women were already squared off with each other. Mommy and Miss Maggie were predicting who was going to do what to who during the funeral services.

"Ain't it a shame! Miss Dottie Louise wants to ride in the family limousine, and Mother Bea won't even let her."

"And why should she? The limousine is for the family. Dottie Louise is not part of the family."

"But they lived together all those years. That should count for something. She cooked and cleaned for him just like she was his wife. Took a few slaps from him, too, so I have heard."

"But she was not his wife, and she knew that his legal wife lived less than a mile from her. Just like Brother Possum knew that the snake was a snake when he picked him up and put him in his pocket, Dottie Louise knew that Frank was a married man. She has no rights to anything of his. It is all Mother Bea's now. If Dottie Lee behaves herself, Mother Bea just might let her go on living in the house. She doesn't have to, but she just might."

"Lord, have mercy! I hope that they don't get into a brawl during the funeral services. You know, a lot of folk are planning to come to the funeral even though Fred didn't attend church regularly. There are always those who come just to "see" who falls out. But now, there are folks planning to come to see who carries on the loudest, and they are hoping to see who "pops" who upside the head first."

Now I wanted to see what was going to happen. As luck would have it, the combined youth and adult choir was requested to sing during the funeral services, and I agreed to sing. This way, I would have a bird's eye view from the safety of the choir stand in case things became tumultuous. Reverend McCarver officiated at the funeral service:

"We are gathered here today to say goodbye to Brother Frank. Ahh, yaas. He wasn't a churchgoing man. He smoked tobacco, gambled, used foul language in public, and drank the devil's brew. Umhummh. But even so, he is a child of the God that we worship. Can I get an *amen*? As he is being laid to rest today, our hearts go out to his wife, Mother Bea and their daughter, Halleylou. Can I get an *amen?* And our hearts also go out to the lady he lived with and her daughter as well. Yes, I had to say it. It is the truth. It is the stone truth, and you all know it!"

I looked over at Mother Bea as she started to rock back and forth humming. "Precious Lord, take my hand ..."

It wasn't time yet, but Shirley and Halleylou both went up to the casket together and appeared to be engaged in a "so you think that you can mourn louder than me" contest. One was screaming, "Daddyyyyy," and the other was screaming, "Daddy Freddddddd!" Ushers were fanning them both and trying to entice them to please take their seats when Shirley tried to remove one of Daddy Fred's cufflinks. At this point, Halleylou leapt upon her with the ferocity of a tiger. It all happened so quickly. Folks heard the vilest of names being called between the two girls. They managed to get in several swipes and claw marks upon each other's faces before two deacons bravely pulled them apart—temporarily. Shirley still had her hand on Fred's wrist, and Halleylou still had her hand dug into Shirley's arm, so it is no wonder that the dead man's arm was pulled out of the casket and sort of just hung in midair. Mother Bea continued humming her song and stood up and started to slowly make her way to the front of the church. "Lead me on, help me stand. I am tired. I am weak. I am worn."

I don't know which girl was responsible, but the first deacon suddenly landed on the floor on his back, and the second deacon landed on top of him. The girls looked like two Tasmanian devils as they whirled about, each trying to significantly beat Brother Fred's love out of the other. Folks saw someone's postiche fly up in the air and land on Brother Fred's extended arm. It sat there perched like a falcon observing the melee. A fake pearl necklace was snatched off someone's neck, and the plastic pearls hit the floor like hail. *Ping. Ping. Ping. PING!* Two pair of legs went up in the air, and everyone could see where someone's fishnet stockings had specks of fingernail polish to stop the thigh-high snags from turning into devastating runs. It took the combined effort of four additional deacons to pull those two girls apart.

The girls were led out to the pastor's study, still crying and intermittently screaming, "Daddyyyyy" and "Daddy Fredddd." Then Miss Dottie Louise started up: "Fred, Fred, Fred, oh no, not my Fred. Not my Fred. Fred, Fred, Fred!" She passed right by the swaying and humming Mother Bea and made her way to the casket and put her arms around the dead man and covered his face with kisses. The ushers tried to remove her, but she would not budge. "Take me with you, darling. Please take me with you." At this point, Mother Bea had made it to the coffin. "Oh, oh!" Everyone held his breath in anticipation of what was about to erupt—World War III? The Apocalypse? Mt. Vesuvius? The Fire This Time? It took six deacons to corral the two girls, and the first two deacons sustained non-life-threatening injuries. Who was going to be able to corral these two women? Who was even going to try?

"Through the day, through the night."

To our surprise, Mother Bea put her arms around Miss Dottie Louise. She hugged her right there at the casket and didn't let go until Miss Dottie Louise calmed down and was humming and swaying in unison with her. Mother Bea then gently led her back to her seat.

"Precious Lord …"

By the time Mother Bea and Miss Dottie Louise had finished humming the song, Miss Dottie Louise had completely settled down and was attentive while the congregation filed past the coffin for one last look at the dearly departed. Mother Bea waited to be the last person to view the remains of Brother Fred. She cried gently and said "Fred, I always loved you." She took out his discarded wedding band from her bosom and placed it back on his finger. Over ten years ago, he had thrown the wedding band in the trash, and she had retrieved it. She had been keeping it for the time when he would return to his senses and come back home after atoning for his sins against her. Then she said her final goodbye to him.

The casket was closed, and the procession began with Mother Bea walking directly behind the coffin. Miss Dottie Louise joined the congregation that filed out of the church and headed for their automobiles to make the trip to the cemetery. The legal family and the live-in family left the church in separate limousines. The cavalcade appeared in this order: the hearse carrying the remains of Brother Fred, followed by a black limousine carrying Mother Bea and her daughter Halleylou, followed by a second black limousine carrying Miss Dottie Louise, church members, family, and friends who had come to pay final respects.

The following Saturday, Mommy and Miss Maggie sent us outside again so that they could "talk" about what had happened without being heard. You know that they were heard because I am now telling you about it.

"Maggie, Mother Bea sure is a woman of strong character and moral fortitude. She demonstrated that!"

"Humph! I would have had Dottie Louise's rotten old carcass thrown out of the church, carrying on that way about a man that was not even hers."

"Mother Bea had compassion for that woman. The mistake that Dottie Louise made was to fall in love with an unavailable man. In any event, she lost someone that she loved too."

"Now, Aurora, if my Arthur acts a fool and leaves me for someone else, she can have his tail when he dies, and she can pay to bury him also. Humph! I wouldn't put up with that mess, not me!"

"It takes strong character and moral fortitude to forgive someone who has participated in hurting you. We may never know what lies Fred told Dottie Louise about Mother Bea."

"Now come on, Aurora. How do you figure that he told Miss Dottie Louise lies about his wife?"

"Have you ever known a married man to tell his girlfriend that his wife is a wonderful woman and that he is the catalyst that dissolved the union? Did you see how Dottie Louise melted when Mother Bea embraced her? That was strength, and Dottie Louise seemed to see Mother Bea in a different light. At that point, I think that Mother Bea forgave Dottie Louise, and she forgave Fred also. That takes strong character and moral fortitude."

"Humph! I would not have forgiven either one of them! Aurora, she should have gone upside Dottie Louise's head!"

"Maggie, the man is dead now. Mother Bea and Dottie Louise are living. They can live on this earth hating each other and being miserable each time they see each other, or they can try to pull things together. There are still two daughters who need guidance and raising."

"And did you see those two show out? Folks thought that perhaps the two women might tie one off, no one even considered those teenaged girls would try to kill each other. Why on earth were they fighting like that?"

"I found out why Halleylou had jumped so viciously upon Shirley during the funeral services. Remember last year when Gensler Lee Diamond Store had a sale on men's diamond cufflinks? Well, last Christmas, both Halleylou and Shirley had bought Fred a pair, unaware that each had procured the same gift for the same man— one for her daddy, and the other for her mother's live-in boyfriend. Shirley wanted to have one of the cufflinks to remember Fred by, so she attempted to take one off his body before they closed the coffin. Halleylou saw this, and in her mind, she remembered the old bicycle that her daddy had found and fixed up for her. She was so proud of it until she saw the new bicycle that Shirley had. Fred would pick up Halleylou and take her shopping for school clothes each year. She would get a pair of shoes and a new outfit to wear on the first day. Shirley always got three new pairs of shoes, and she had a new outfit to sport daily for the first two weeks of school. On her birthday, Fred always got Halleylou a real nice toy and some ice cream to go with the cake that Mother Bea would make for her. One year, he even got her a puppy. That same year, Fred took Dottie Louise, Shirley, and some of her friends to Frontier Village for Shirley's birthday. They invited Halleylou, but she didn't want to go. Now, in her mind, Shirley was trying to steal something precious that she had given to her daddy, and Halleylou planned for her daddy to take the cufflinks to heaven with him. She was willing to fight to prevent the theft from occurring right in front of her eyes. Shirley's mother had 'stolen' her daddy from her mother. Shirley had stolen his heart, or so she thought. Halleylou was not going to let Shirley 'steal' the last Christmas gift that she had given him."

"Oh, that was what it was all about. I would have stomped a hole in her butt too, taking jewelry off of my dead daddy! Humph!"

"Maggie girl, you have got to have faith, and you have to stand up and do what is right even when someone you love has hurt you. Look at everyone now: The girls loved Frank, but they will be more careful about who they choose to share their lives with. They witnessed firsthand the frustration and pain that goes hand in hand with an illicit relationship. Mother Bea agreed to let Dottie Louise rent the house for one year before she sells the property. Then Dottie Louise will have to find somewhere else to stay. Mother Bea received the assets that were in the bank, and she is also receiving Fred's pension check. No more 'bottom of the sack' drop-offs for her and her daughter. Dottie Louise receives nothing. Dottie Louise has to get out and get a job in order to pay Mother Bea the rent, buy food, and pay for the utilities. Mother Bea has released the anger and pain that Fred's abandonment caused her. Dottie Louise is looking for someone else to take Fred's place. How sad that she feels so poorly about herself that she lowers herself to the relationship choices that do not favor her in life and certainly will not favor her in the hereafter. What she is going through now is far worse than any whooping that Mother Bea could have given her.

"And the kicker! Everyone knew that Mother Bea had adopted Halleylou. What we did not know was that Halleylou was Fred's biological daughter. Fred and Mother Bea had opened their home to foster children when they learned that Mother Bea would never be able to conceive. The biological mother of Halleylou was one of the teenage girls given shelter in Brother Fred and Mother Bea's home! The teenaged mother had left her newborn child in the hospital and moved out of state. Mother Bea had put Brother Fred out and taken the child, legally adopted her and raised her as her own. She had told Brother Fred that he could not come back home until he got down on his knees in church and asked the Lord for forgiveness. When he refused to do that, she told everyone that he had left her. What Fred had done was to take out a life insurance policy for Halleylou, and he had stored it with a copy of the original birth certificate in a safe deposit box at Crocker Citizen's Bank.

The instructions were that Halleylou be told the truth about her conception, and she would be able to attain the $50,000 proceeds from the life insurance policy at the age of twenty-one. What do you think about that? Halleylou was upset about birthday parties, bicycles, and new school clothes, but her father left her something that he considered far more valuable."

CHAPTER 37

Cleo

LaDONNA WAS A PECULIAR CHILD. At the age of twelve, she still sucked her thumb and slept with her parents. She was still playing with baby dolls and stuffed animals while the rest of her peers at church had graduated to 45 records, *Bronze Thrills* magazines, and sneaking to put on lipstick. LaDonna would come to the youth choir rehearsal and sing her heart out, but she would not engage in the girlish chatter with the rest of us afterwards. We just figured that she was peculiar.

The spring of our eighth-grade year, LaDonna stopped coming to the youth choir rehearsal and the BTU meetings as well. Her mother told us that LaDonna had a problem with her glands and would need to undergo an operation in another city since the nearest specialist was there. We all made cards for LaDonna wishing her well with her surgery and prayers for her speedy recovery.

LaDonna came back home that summer. She had gained some weight, probably due to the gland surgery, and she took up where she had left off with youth choir rehearsal and BTU. Her parents had adopted an infant while she was gone. Her mother told everyone that the infant was a relative whose mother had not lived past childbirth. People in the church began to suspect that the infant was LaDonna's baby and the well-meaning Christian-centered folk began to whisper about LaDonna, and their whisperings were menacingly reiterated by their youth choir family members.

"Humph! You know that baby belongs to LaDonna. They are just lying about a dead relative to protect her."

"My mama says that she is supposed to get down on her knees before the church and ask for forgiveness for her sin."

"My mama says that she can no longer sing in the youth choir with us. She needs to move on into the adult choir where she belongs."

"The church needs to put them all out, lying like that!"

LaDonna just pretended that she did not hear these totally auditory statements and continued to come to church and sing with her heart. That all stopped the day her maternal grandmother, Mother Mary, brought the police to church to arrest LaDonna's parents. Her complaint was that the stepfather had given LaDonna the baby—not some dead relative in another town. Mother Mary cried that she had protested about the way that they were raising LaDonna, and no one listened to her. They claimed that she was just an old woman with crazy thoughts in her head. She had begged her daughter not to marry Joel. He had just shown up in Vallejo from out of nowhere, claiming to have no live family anywhere. LaDonna was just a little girl when her mother and Joel married, around five or six. The family had lived with Mother Mary for the first five years of their marriage because Joel had a hard time finding and keeping a job. During this time, Mother Mary had noticed things that were not proper. Joel knew better than to hit her daughter in front of her, but she noticed that when LaDonna would get scared at night, she would crawl into bed with her mother and stepfather. The practice continued into LaDonna's puberty, and the more Mother Mary complained about it, the more estranged she and her daughter (LaDonna's mother) became. Finally, the family moved out, and Mother Mary only saw her granddaughter on Sundays in church.

The day that Mother Mary brought the police to church was the first Sunday in August, and the youth choir had just finished singing when they entered the sanctuary. The police spoke briefly to the pastor, and then the pastor asked the entire family to meet with him in his office. There, the arrests were made, and LaDonna and the baby were released to Mother Mary. All this, and the pastor made it back to the pulpit in time to officiate the monthly communion amidst inquisitive looks and whispers throughout the congregation.

That stepfather went to jail, and we never saw him again. Rumor had it that he had been convicted of child molestation more than once in another state. That could be why he just "showed up" in Vallejo. He needed somewhere to be where folks did not know of him. He met and married a gullible woman with a young daughter—both of whom he could control with the menace of his fist and his penis.

The mother received probation. She went back to live with her mother, LaDonna, and the baby. They all lived together until LaDonna graduated from high school the same year that I did. She enlisted in one the military branches, left Vallejo with her child, and she never came back.

I always felt that LaDonna was dealt with unfairly by that congregation and by the person who was supposed to protect her—her mother. The whispers behind her back and blatant statements made within her hearing about her "sins" and how she had yet to get on her knees in front of the church and beg for forgiveness were repugnant to me. Some of the pseudo self-righteous ones actually wanted her to display this humbleness before she would be allowed to take communion on the first Sunday! How could they slap her in the face like that! LaDonna was the victim! Her stepfather should have had his testicles cauterized, and her mother should have been sent to a mental institution. What type of mother would allow her husband to sexually assault her own daughter in her marital bed with her sleeping next to her or pretending to sleep while this atrociousness was taking place? Those pious church folk talked about LaDonna so bad, but they accepted her mother when she came to church laid out in the latest fashion complete with furs, leather, and diamonds. I heard that she was quite generous with her monthly tithes also. No one suggested that her mother get down on her knees in front of the church and beg for forgiveness. Her story was that she did not know what was going on. Hah! The grandmother deflated that pusillanimous lie. She had argued with that mother for years for allowing LaDonna to sleep in the bed nestled between her and her husband, all to no avail.

When the mother got tired of hearing about how inappropriately she was raising her daughter, she and her family moved out of the grandmother's house.

The reality of the dichotomy of acceptance for a "sin" in that church began to drive a wider wedge in my aura of respect and disdain for the Baptist Church. I had witnessed women in the church flirting with married men, and I had witnessed men in the church eyeing married women. There was a deacon who had slapped a woman in the face during a business meeting for daring to disagree with him. There was a choir pianist who routinely removed her dress before putting on her choir robe. She would get all riled up during a song and "fall out" on the floor with her robe unzipped, displaying her underwear. The head deacon was a known alcoholic. The pastor's wife once brandished a handgun during a heated business meeting because some members of the congregation were questioning pastoral expenditures that did not make sense to them. There was one tenured minister who was reputed to have up to four children by women in the church other than his wife, and no one made any of these folks get down on their knees and ask for forgiveness. I needed a break from this hypocrisy. I began to go to catechism with Ranethia.

CHAPTER 38

Cleophus

I AM MY OWN SELF man, and I know that I am sick. I have been sick for a very long time. I tried to help myself, and I have been well enough during the past fifty or so years to know when to admit myself into the hospital. I admitted myself into the hospital so that I would not hurt the people I love the most—my wife and children. The United States Air Force did not know how to medically treat me! They wanted to give me medications, and before I took them, I did the research on them. I was not about to let them make me into a second-stage guinea pig like they did the Tuskegee airmen. Each time they recommended a "cocktail," I looked up everything that was available on each of the ingredients. One of them caused metabolic changes in the patient. I refused to take that one. Another had the potential for cognitive and motor damages. I refused to take that one. Another one could cause cerebrovascular adverse reactions like a stroke. There was no way in hell that I was going to let them experiment on me with that one. The list went on and on. When they claimed that they had found the perfect "cocktail" for me, I discovered that it was associated with neuroleptic malignant symptom, also known as NMS, and could cause life-threatening fever and an altered mental status. No, I did not let them give that one to me either.

I did go to the counseling sessions, both private and group. During the private counseling sessions, I made a point of blowing the psychologist's mind away with the realm of my mind. They would write in their reports that I was deceptive, would not open up to them, would not admit obvious shortcomings. Hell! Who needed those psychologists? I didn't! I knew better than to let them in on my "inside" thoughts. They would only use it against me, and I was not about to help them to do that. So I just played along with them.

The group counseling sessions were actually quite entertaining. I would sit there and appear to be either amused or saddened by the life stories that were shared there. These stories ranged from witnessing firsthand buddies killed during combat, cheating wives, strange children at home whose births did not add up to when the husbands had last had a furlough, deaths of family members, disrespectful treatment, the lack of nonmilitary jobs post-military discharge, dead dogs, male rapes on base, substance abuse, etc. I would sit quietly until someone noticed that I had not "shared" yet. To keep the peace, I would share some cockamamie story about a recurring dream that I was having. I told them that it was such a vivid dream, that I was sometimes afraid to go to sleep. To solve my problem, I relayed I would set my clock to ring every two hours to keep me from getting into deep sleep. I had learned from my research on sleep stages that most vivid dreams happen in this stage. Since I was feigning fear of recurring dreams, I had the perfect excuse. No deep sleep, no recurring dream. This would keep them mesmerized and off my case at least for a little while.

I decided to cure myself, and I began to read everything I could put my hands on about schizophrenia. I learned that many veterans also find therapy or counseling to be a great help when dealing with the symptoms of schizophrenia. Cognitive behavioral therapy can help you learn ways to deal with your symptoms. Counseling can also help you improve your personal relationships and manage schizophrenia symptoms so they interfere less with your everyday life. You and your family might find it helpful to attend family support groups to work on strategies for dealing with the stress of schizophrenia.

In addition to treatment, you can adjust your lifestyle to help manage schizophrenia symptoms. When recovering from schizophrenia, you should do the following:

- Only use drugs prescribed by your doctor, and take your medicine as prescribed.
  - ○ I will not take the drugs!
- Avoid excessive alcohol use, or don't drink alcohol at all.
  - ○ I drink three to four beers each day, and I am not going to stop! Hah!
- Adopt an active and healthy lifestyle by eating right and exercising.
  - ○ This I can do. I am in perfect shape.
- Find ways to reduce stress in your life.
  - ○ I am trying, but I believe that my wife's first husband is trying to win her back even though they say that he is dead. I don't believe it.
  - ○ My wife is getting fat. She doesn't look the way she did when I first saw her.
  - ○ I didn't want all those kids! I only wanted my own son whom I named Junior. She tricked me and had all those kids!
  - ○ Slapping Aurora across her face is a stress reliever.
  - ○ Sometimes, I am afraid that I will kill my entire family and then myself. When I feel like that, I check myself into the hospital. Here I am.
- Get the right amount of sleep.
  - ○ I can sleep when I feel like it, and I can wake up without an alarm clock.

Even severe symptoms of schizophrenia can be controlled with good treatment. However, symptoms can still occur while receiving treatment, so an ongoing relationship with a doctor will help you make any needed adjustments. Schizophrenia is a chronic condition that requires ongoing management.

There was one doctor that I had begun to trust at Travis Air Force Base, and he and I agreed on a course of treatment for me: no medications, vitamins, diet, no alcohol (hah!), regular PT (physical training), eight hours of sleep each day, individual and group counseling. I agreed to check back into the hospital whenever life became too anxiety driven. I was able to leave the hospital and go home whenever I wanted to.

I spent countless hours in the medical library. Schizophrenia was identified as a severe brain disorder in which people interpret reality abnormally. I don't care what the doctors believe; I did not interpret reality abnormally. I knew when people were plotting and planning behind my back. The literature claimed that alcohol can conflict with the positive effects of schizophrenic medication. That would present no problem to me because I was not going to take the medication. What do you think about that? Hah! I pored over the schizophrenic topics published by the Schizophrenia International Research Society (SIRS), the American Psychological Association (APA), the American Medical Association (AMA), and the American Psychological Society (APS). I probably knew more about the disorder than anyone on the base did, and that included the physicians.

Stuart kept me abreast of everything that was going on with Aurora and the kids. He had an apartment just across the street, and he could see and hear everything that went on in that house. Stuart could hear the kids splashing bath water. Stuart could smell Aurora's cooking. Stuart could see her watching the stories on television while she ironed if he just happened to walk down the alley at the appropriate time. Stuart let me know that from time to time, she let that gook, Mrs. Do, come into my kitchen for coffee and chatter even though I expressly forbade that woman coming onto the property. Stuart could hear Aurora singing gospel songs, gossiping on the telephone, and he could see her and the kids when they walked to and from church each Sunday. His eyes, his nose, and his ears were needed to keep me in charge of what was going on in that house! I knew that Doc Henry was just waiting for the opportunity to steal Aurora back, and I was not going to let that happen.

Aurora, as pretty and smart as she was, was also very gullible. She would try to do whatever I told her to do. I had trained her that way. When she disobeyed me, a sharp slap to the face would bring her back to reality. That is how my daddy trained my mother, and it worked for him. Once, Aurora had rummaged through my locked trunk and come across my Glock. She had taken the bullets out and called herself hiding them by burying them in the backyard. I scared her shitless when during an argument, I got that Glock, pointed it at her head, and pulled the trigger! She didn't know that I already knew there were no bullets in it! Boy, did she skedaddle out of the house that day! I never had another problem with her going through my locked trunk or opening my mail after that. See, even the pretty ones can be taught a lesson they will never forget. What do you think about that! Hah!

The day that I decided to really leave my family, I have to admit that I was out of control. I can't even remember what Aurora and I were fighting about, but when I had given her the traditional slap across the face, she had thrown a lamp at me! Women are to be protected and cared for—they are not supposed to fight back! I had to really whip her tail that night. I made a point of tearing up the furniture to scare her back to her senses. I threw her against a couple of walls and dragged her around the kitchen by that long hair of hers. My oldest daughter had run up to me and yelled at me to leave her mother alone. I just swept her into the wall in the living room with one sweep of my arm so I could continue with my own self business of chastising my own self wife. Then Cleodine did the unforgiveable! She picked up the telephone and was attempting to call the white man on me! Here I was in my own self house with my own self family, and she was calling the white man on me! Visions of fat white men dragging me by my neck, colored men hanging from trees in the woods, refusals of credit, Mr. Baxter slapping little Melody across her face so hard that she flipped over backward, Brother dead, living on the banks of the Sowashee Creek, segregated living quarters, chain gangs, and frontline exposure in the military guided my right hand as it snatched the telephone from her and slammed it against her head! She just lay there on the floor. Oh my god! Had I killed her?

When the police released me the next day, it was with the under-standing that I was going back to Travis Air Force Base to check back into the hospital. Instead, I went by the house to see my children for probably the last time. The babysitter was there, and I asked her to iron a fresh shirt for me. I gave her some money to give to Aurora until I could get settled, and then I left via a Yellow Taxi Cab.

They tell me that I was found wandering alone in Van Cortlandt Park in the Bronx with nothing more than the clothes I had on my back, my military ID, and $200,000 cash sewn into the lining of my coat. They put me in the hospital, and they administered the antipsy-chotic drugs that I had avoided for so many years.

CHAPTER 39

Cleo

IT WAS 1996, AND I had so much to be thankful for. At forty-six years of age, I had attained three college degrees: BA in behavioral science, MA in counseling, and doctorate in educational leadership. I had a beautiful Shappell trilevel home nestled in the foothills of Silicon Valley. I had a wonderful job as the principal of a middle school in one of the top-paying school districts in Northern California. I was an officer in the local chapter of my sorority, Alpha Kappa Alpha Sorority Inc. My son was doing well with a wife and three lovely and intelligent children, and I was starting to gather together my short stories for an eventual publication. As I was reflecting upon my life and the blessings from God that I had received, I began to reflect on my anger toward my father. He was absent most of my growing-up years, and the times he was home were marred with fear and hostility because I had seen him hit my mother. Something warm and soothing came over me that day as I sat at the computer. It was the afternoon of July 19, 1966, when I decided to try to locate my father. There were websites that advertised how to look for lost relatives and friends. I previewed a number of them and selected one that focused upon lost black family members. I posted this message:

> I am trying to locate my father, Mr. Cleophus George Duarté, who left California in 1962. He may be residing in New York since he has

maintained a post office box there, but we really do not know. My father is about 5' 10" tall, dark-complexioned and wears glasses. He was in the United States Air Force for a number of years. He is originally from Newton, Mississippi, but he could be residing in any state in the union. I am all grown up now, and he may not want to see me, but he needs to know that he has a grandson, a great-grandson, and two great-granddaughters that he might like to get to know. If you know of such a person, please have him contact me at ...

For so many years, I had wanted to find my father just so that I could sock him in the nose and slap him hard across the cheek in remembrance of what I saw him do to my mother. Because of what I experienced from his assaultive behavior witnessed as a child, I was ready to take the life of the man that I married when he assaulted me. I felt this way even after I had completed my first two degrees in college, which focused upon abnormal behavior and counseling techniques. I felt that my father had gotten away with demoralizing and beating my mother, and I wanted to pay him back for all that I had witnessed and all that the family Duarté had gone through in his absence. God is so good! As soon as I posted that query, I actually forgave him for all the treacherous things that I felt he had done, and I forgave myself for holding on to that anger all those years. I felt such a release of pent-up anger and hostility when I posted that message. The anger and hostility that I had felt for decades just melted like butter on a baked potato fresh from the oven.

The call from his attorney came about two weeks later. My father had died of a massive heart attack. He had been living in a veteran's home in the Bronx in New York. The attorney was trying to locate his beneficiaries. He had left an estate valued at over a million dollars in stock, and he had willed it to his children. He had died on July 19, 1996.

CHAPTER 40

Cleo

I GAVE MYSELF THE OPPORTUNITY to meet my father's youngest brother. I scoured the internet for Duarté surnames. I knew that he had siblings in Mississippi, New York, and Chicago. I was scheduled to attend a Boulé in Chicago, so that would be my opportunity to look up this relative I had never met before. I started by scouring Chicago. I knew that a player with the last name of Duarté was playing for the Chicago Bears. Ooh, what if he was a relative of mine? The eighth call that I made was to an Arnold Duarté. It was him! He acknowledged that he had a brother named Cleophus and that their family was from a town called Newton, Mississippi. We made plans to meet the next day. He was going to pick me up at the Chicago Convention Center and drive me to his home where the family would have a fish fry. This would give me a chance to meet my relatives. The next day, I was waiting at the appointed spot, but I never did see the van that he had described. I thought, hmm, abandonment must run in the family. I didn't bother to try to call him, and he didn't call me either. My convention roommate, Judy, insisted that I call him the next day.

"You came all the way here to Chicago, and you need to make every effort to see your father's family."

So I called the next day. It seems that we were on opposite sides of that great big convention center. I was waiting in front of the hotel that was adjacent to the convention center, and he was downstairs at the entrance to the convention center. Traffic control would not let him park anywhere. He was frustrated, and I was frustrated. He offered to come and get me at the hotel, but I insisted on taking a taxicab. When I arrived at his home, he paid the taxi driver and took me inside to meet his wife, and then he drove us over to the home of his youngest sister, Melody. We talked long and hard. Melody told me of how she had called my father Buddy, and of how he had protected her while she was growing up. He was her hero and favorite of the siblings. I told them that my father had passed on, and I told them of how he never wanted us to come to the south.

Arnold said, "He didn't want you to know about what happened down there."

Melody spoke up, "No need to bring that up now."

"Yes, there is. She deserves to know," Arnold countered. He then told me the following facts: "Our father, Scripture, routinely beat on our mother. Our mother routinely physically chastised the older children, Stuart [Brother], Cleophus [Buddy] and Evelyn [Sister]. The three older children routinely beat on the six younger ones. Everybody beat on somebody in that house."

Melody broke in and said, "Everyone in the family beat on the ones below them. I loved Buddy so much because he would protect me not only against the older siblings but against our father when he was in an urge to whoop. Buddy would take my whooping in place of me many a time."

"That day, Melody had to fill in on a job for Sister, who had taken ill. She didn't do the job to the satisfaction of the lady who had hired her, and she had stomped her foot and sassed the lady when she complained."

"It was about some washing and ironing," Melody interjected.

"That white lady's husband drove out to our house and started to raise hell about Melody sassing his wife. He slapped Melody so hard across her face that she flipped backward out of her chair and hit the floor. Buddy jumped up and punched that man square in his jaw, knocking him to the floor. The man had brought a shotgun into the house with him, and he was reaching for it when Buddy grabbed it first, aimed it at the man, and pulled the trigger. It all seemed like it took place in slow motion, but Brother moved in front of Buddy to wrestle away the shotgun, and he was killed. That same round hit both Brother and the white man. They both were killed on the spot."

"Oh my god," I exclaimed.

"That was what he did not want you children and your mother to know, and that is why he kept y'all away from Mississippi and away from the family all those years."

"What did you say his brother's name was, the one who was killed?"

"His name was Stuart."

CHAPTER 41

Cleo

I HAD A LOT OF things to put into perspective. My father had accidentally killed his oldest brother, and this brother's name was Stuart. How had he managed to establish his closest relationship with a friend who had the same name as his deceased brother? A friend who had been his constant companion from the days on the Sowashee Creek bank, to enlistment in the United States Air Force, to being stationed at Hamilton Field Air Force Base and Travis Air Force Base at the same time? This close friend who was his confidante and who spied on Mommy whenever he was away from the home? How come none of us had ever really seen or talked to this Stuart?

After my father's death, Mommy had told us the truth about the times he was "away" on Air Force business. He had suffered a mental breakdown and spent most of his time in the hospital at Travis Air Force base in the psychological ward. The times that he came home, he had actually earned a family pass so that he could spend time with his family. The agreement was that whenever the anxieties were getting out of control, he would check himself back into the hospital. He did not want our mother to know the background of his illness, and the Air Force respected his wishes. They never told her the truth about his condition, and after his death, they still hemmed and hawed about releasing his medical records to her. To this date, they have never released the confidential information.

He never told her what had really happened in Mississippi. When his mother passed, he had gone to Newton, Mississippi, for the funeral, but he did not stay very long. He told Mommy that folks at the church were whispering to each other about him, so he left as quickly as he had arrived. Arnold confirmed this when he told me that people were astonished to see him after so many years since the double shootings. They were looking at him and whispering, "There he is. That is the one that done it."

I earned a bachelor's degree in behavioral science, master's degree in counseling and a doctorate degree in educational leadership. Daddy had always implored us to "get your education. It is something that they can never take away from you." All my research studies and training clarified for me that my father was probably suffering from schizophrenia, a bipolar disorder, or a combination of both. Stuart (the close friend) never existed except in my father's mind. He was created by my father's subconscious after the shock of Brother's death.

Schizophrenia is a serious brain illness. People who have it may hear voices that aren't there. They may think other people are trying to hurt them. Sometimes they don't make sense when they talk. The disorder makes it hard for them to keep a job or take care of themselves. Symptoms of schizophrenia usually start between ages sixteen and thirty. Men often develop symptoms at a younger age than women. People usually do not get schizophrenia after age forty-five. There are three types of symptoms:

1. Psychotic symptoms distort a person's thinking. These include hallucinations (hearing or seeing things that are not there), delusions (beliefs that are not true), trouble organizing thoughts, and strange movements.
2. "Negative" symptoms make it difficult to show emotions and to function normally. A person may seem depressed and withdrawn.
3. Cognitive symptoms affect the thought process. These include trouble using information, making decisions, and paying attention.

No one is sure what causes schizophrenia. Genes, environment, and brain chemistry may play a role. There is no cure. Medicine can help control many of the symptoms. The patient may need to try different medicines to see which works best. The patient should stay on the medicine for as long as the doctor recommends. Additional treatments can help the patient deal with the illness from day to day.

As I pored over the information related to schizophrenia, I saw evidence of the symptoms in my father's behavior.

1. People who have it may hear voices that aren't there.
    *   My father had conversations with this Stuart character that no one else ever saw or heard.
    *   He claimed that someone was watching our home and reporting the various goings on to him.

2. They may think other people are trying to hurt them.
    *   My father believed that the neighbors were all trying to "see what he was doing." I thought that his hatred of Korean, German, Italian, and anybody Caucasian was due to his experience in the military. Maybe it was.
    *   But he believed that the Negroes were jealous of him and "out to get him" as well. Hence, I do not remember any friends of his ever coming to the house to visit.
    *   He never trusted my mother. He believed that she was plotting to leave him and reunite with her first husband. He sought to control every aspect of her life (friends, finances, communications, etc.) to thwart her attempts to take his money and leave him all alone. Hence, he physically assaulted her when she did not agree with him, spent too much money, opened his mail, spent too much time away from home, did not cook what he wanted to eat, did not clean the house to his specifications, or dared to have coffee with the Korean neighbor who lived down the alley.
    *   When my father threw me against the wall and later slammed the telephone against my head, he was pro-

tecting himself from what I was attempting to do—call the white men (police) to come and get him.

3. Symptoms of schizophrenia usually start between ages sixteen and thirty.
    •   My father was seventeen years of age when the tragedy occurred with his brother Stuart. Shortly after Stuart's death, the "other" Stuart appeared.
    •   The second Stuart was his confidante and counseled him from the time that he was on the banks of the Sowashee Creek until he died at the age of eighty-eight. This "other" Stuart looked out for him and protected him, kind of like what a big brother would do.

4. "Negative" symptoms make it difficult to show emotions and to function normally.
    •   I don't remember my father ever hugging me or kissing me.
    •   I don't remember my father ever tucking me in the bed at night.
    •   I don't remember my father ever telling me that I was pretty, smart, or talented. He once made fun of me for trying to sing the song made famous by Della Reese, "Don't You Know." I was about nine years old, and he said that she looked and sounded like a man, and so did I. I never sang out again, not even when I was in the children's choir at church. To this day, I still do not sing out in church.
    •   I don't remember my father ever telling me that he loved me.

Knowing what I now know about schizophrenia, I can just imagine the way my father must have suffered! Mommy once said to me that she thought that in spite of his actions, he really did love us. She wished the United States Air Force had taught her how to live with him. Instead, she lived in fear until she had the emotional strength to accept that he was not going to change.

The attorney who contacted us upon his death told me that he had been assigned to be my father's consigliere (counselor) when he showed up on the streets of New York with over two hundred thousand dollars cash sewn in the lining of his coat, his military ID, and no idea of who he was or where he had been. Thus began a friendship/relationship that spanned more than three decades. The attorney told me that my father would spend time in the veterans' hospital in the Bronx in New York, start feeling better, and get out for a trial independent living. During these trials, he would visit the attorney every week when he came to pick up his mail. They drank coffee and talked about the stock market and his experiences in the US military. When my father started to feel the old anxieties and discomforts coming back, he would check himself back into the veterans' hospital. The attorney thinks that something that happened to my father in the military was the root cause of his mental problems. That military experience could have played a significant role in his dissociative personality issues, but I believe it was the tragic death of his older brother that was the root cause. Anything else that happened, including the racial discrimination he experienced while in the military, just added on to trauma already in existence.

My father lived quite well when he was on independent living, making successful trades on the New York Stock Exchange, playing billiards at the veterans' home, where he resided whenever he was not in the hospital, reading and discussing finances with his friend, the attorney, who also served as his counselor. The attorney encouraged him to fly out to California to visit his children when he had the first of three heart attacks. He chose not to, stating that he was afraid to fly and disliked both the train and the Greyhound. He later admitted that he was afraid that he might hurt someone. He had been gone for so long, and Stuart had advised him that the folks in Vallejo would point at him and whisper about him. No, he was not going to California. What he chose to do was to establish a last will and testament, leaving his entire estate to his children. In the will, he claimed that he did not have a wife.

For so many years, I had bitter feelings toward my father, and I was glad that he was not around. My childhood memories are marked with hearing and seeing the vicious way that he brutally attacked my mother. I used to think of ways that I would seek him out when I was all grown up, and I would slap him across the face as hard as I could in revenge for the way he treated my mother. I believe that the skillet of frying potatoes that I threw at Junior was also aimed for him. I had experienced my father beating my mother, and I had experienced Junior beating me. When I threw that skillet, I was throwing my pent-up anger at the source of physical admonitions that should never have occurred. After that incident, Junior never hit me again. I only had to mention the word *skillet*, and he would stop being the bully that he had turned into.

When the attorney first contacted us to inform us that our father had died and left an inheritance, Junior had the nerve to tell me that he should receive the majority of the funds (over one million dollars) because he was our father's eldest child, he was named after him, and he needed it more than anyone else. He said that he would buy Mommy a new car but that she did not need anything else. After all, she had her own home that was paid for, and she had a pension check coming from the state of California every month for her years of employment at Sonoma State Hospital. Mommy did not agree to that. The attorney told her that she could have either two-thirds of the proceeds or one-half of the proceeds. The children would get the rest. Mommy opted to take one half, with the other half going to the offspring. That did not set well with Junior. Mommy called me in tears one day and told me that Junior had hired an attorney to fight her. The lawyer claimed that he had proof that Mommy had abandoned the marriage in 1956 and therefore was not entitled to any of the proceeds from her husband's estate. I called Junior to find out why he was doing this to her. His answer was that he needed the money more than she did, and he would do whatever it took to get it.

"You are the only one of us who is just sitting on your behind and not working for a living. You ought to be ashamed of yourself harassing our mother like that. You got one more time for her to call me crying about something that you have done, and I am coming to Vallejo with my skillet. Do you understand me?"

I slammed down the phone. He called me back within two minutes.

"I am disabled, and I need the money to take care of myself. That is all I am trying to get her to see. What you think about that, huh?"

The attorney let Junior know that, yes, Mommy had filed for a divorce in 1956, but it was never completed. I remember Mommy telling me that she had filed for divorce right after we came back from the state of Washington. She cancelled the process because she was pregnant with my younger sister, Karol Ann. Junior's claim was dismissed because Mommy was still my father's legal spouse at the time of his death. Neither the state of New York nor California will allow one spouse to disinherit the other spouse. Case closed.

My studies in Behavioral Science, Counseling and Education reverberated in my mind as I contemplated the impact of my father's illness on the family and how things may have been different if my mother only knew how to successfully live with him. How might the lives of my siblings and I have been different under different circumstances?

Research has shown that children who witness domestic violence tend to be more aggressive and anxious than children from non-violent homes, and they are less likely to be successful in school and social activities.

- Hmm, Cleophus Jr. was not successful in school and he blatantly separated himself from positive social activities.
- I can see how anxiety played a large role in the relationships that I have had most of my life. I was always preparing for an exit in the event that things became uncomfortable for me.

These children are at higher risk for delinquent behavior, separation anxiety, developmental regression, and sleep problems, including nightmares.

- Cleophus Jr. exhibited delinquent behavior from the age of twelve.

- I on the other hand, had sleep problems. I still suffer with Sleep Apnea. As a child, I used to dream that I had died and was able to float all over town looking in on anyone that I chose. I always had to return to my body within a certain amount of time or the death would be a reality. Could this have been representative of the nightmares referred to in the research on children who witness domestic violence?

Children who have not observed the incident are usually aware of the violence even when others believe they were asleep or otherwise engaged.

- My sister was asleep during the incidences of physical abuse—or was she? As an adult in her 50's, she shared with me that she knew all about it. She was never a delinquent, has never commented about sleep problems—but she is highly anxiety driven, and she frequently detaches herself from the rest of the family for periods of time that have amounted to years.

Understanding the mental/emotional predicament my father was in brought me to a new realization. I realized that while Junior exhibited some of our father's same traits of intelligence, shrewdness, nervousness, incessant smoking, daily consumption of alcohol, distrust of people who considered themselves to be his friends, distrust of women, and the belief that people were out trying to get him, my life's path could have taken a similar journey.

- My father had witnessed his father physically abuse his mother. I witnessed my father physically abuse my mother.
- My father tried to protect his younger sister, Melody. I tried to protect my mother.
- My father had in a fit of rage taken a shotgun to the man who had struck his younger sister in the face. I took a skillet with frying potatoes and threw it at the person who had struck me in the face!

- His brother lost his life because of his rage. My brother and my husband could have lost their lives because of my rage.

What if that cast-iron skillet had connected with Junior's head! Would I have created a make-believe brother named Junior to be my constant companion over the next sixty years?

What if I had made it to Fremont to get the firearm from Diedre? Would I have used it to remove the life force from my own abusive husband?

What if Mommy had been strong enough to fight my father back? Would he have left her alone, or would he have eventually killed her rather than lose control over her?

What if the United Air Force had come clean with my mother and given her the information that she had requested? Could she have learned to support my father in his illness and thus, we all could have lived together as a cohesive family unit?

What if my father could have experienced the joy of seeing his children heed his teachings and "get the education" that he preached?

What if my father had maintained a presence in our lives as we were growing up? Junior might have turned out differently with a father to comfort and guide him through his own anxieties associated with growing up as a man of color in America.

What if my father had turned to prayers instead of beatings when the anxieties of life began to overtake him? Would he have not died alone in a veterans' home?

What if? What if? What if? What if? What if? What if?

How do you successfully mold other people so that they can exemplify the end result that you desire? How much of your own history and family traditions do you incorporate into your decision-making process? How do you differentiate the history and family traditions you have chosen to maintain and the ones you will leave in the past? Do you pray the stubbornness out of them? Do you beat it out of them? Which method works best? A method consisting of prayers, beatings, or a supplication of *prayers and beatings*?

Epilogue

THE INMATES RECEIVED MY FAMILY'S story well. They sat there in silence for what seemed like an eternity before asking, "Dr. Cleo, why are you here?"

I recounted for them that day when I was going to the Kaiser Medical Center to pick up some prescriptions. I saw an elderly woman in the parking lot who appeared to be disoriented and wandering. I stopped my vehicle, rolled down the window, and I asked her if I could help her. She reminded me of Mrs. Do, our Korean neighbor who lived down the alley of my childhood.

"No English," she had said. She then pointed to a younger man who was walking toward her. I figured that this man must be her son, so I went ahead and parked my car. As I was walking toward the medical center, I heard him yelling at her, calling her stupid for not staying where he told her to stay. He was pointing his finger in her face and yelling the way someone would yell at a pet dog for depositing fecal matter on the front lawn.

"Don't talk to your mother like that!" I said to him as I passed him.

"You mind your own damn business. I am not talking to you!"

"It is apparent to me that she got lost. She doesn't deserve to be yelled at like that."

"I said for you to mind your own damn business, you asshole!"

"Okay, I will mind my own damn business, and if you continue to yell at her like that, it will become the business of the police. The state of California takes a dim view on people who abuse elders. I will report you."

"Take a look in the mirror and report yourself, you asshole!"

He looked like he was going to come toward me, so I quickly headed back for my car, got in and turned on the engine. My plan was to drive to the front of the Kaiser Medical Center's main building, park in the no-parking zone, go in, and call for assistance. I had already backed the car out of the parking space and switched the gears to "drive" when I saw him strike that little old lady in her face with his fist! He struck her so hard that she fell backwards, hitting her head on a parked car before falling to the ground bleeding. I don't know where she came from, but I saw a woman who resembled Aunt Willetta stumbling between two parked cars, yelling for him to "stop it," and making a beeline for this horrid man with her pocketbook raised high in weaponry stance to bust him upside the head. In complete terror, I saw him raise what looked like a handgun aimed toward her. "Oh, hell no!" I had visions of my father relentlessly beating my mother, slamming a telephone against my head for having the audacity to call for help, pointing a Glock at her, and totally terrorizing my childhood as I slammed on the accelerator and drove straight for that hateful man, hitting him and knocking him at least four feet into the air. When he landed on the pavement, he moved no more.

The court hearing was brief. I pleaded "no contest" to aggravated assault and voluntary manslaughter. The old lady who had feigned, "No English," spoke very clearly when she described how I had singled her son out and murdered him with my vehicle. She claimed that he had not yelled at her and had never struck her. According to her, there was no provocation for my murderous attack, and I needed to pay for destroying the life of the son who was taking care of her. When my attorney asked the reason for her obvious injuries, she claimed that she fell against a car when I ran her son down in cold blood. No gun was ever found. No witness came forth, including the woman who resembled Aunt Willetta. The prosecution attorney claimed that since the woman I knew as Aunt Willetta had passed away in 1997, I was either making up the eyewitness story or having hallucinations. I refused to even consider an insanity defense because I am not insane. I was fully in control of my thoughts and actions then as I am now. I allowed my rage and fear to take steps to end a man's life. I was ready to accept my punishment for my deed.

I received a sixteen-year sentence for aggravated assault and voluntary manslaughter. I was placed here at the California Women's Correctional Institute in Chino, where I am earning "early release" points for leading one of the therapy groupings. I am a model prisoner, and I hope to be paroled in another couple of years. I will start over.

I had to learn how to appease these folks who think they know me better than I know myself. I am the most educated of the prisoners, and I am now one of the trustees. I get to have my own private lodgings. I get to wear regular clothing. I get to teach classes, and I get to compose my life story for publication. I do not drink coffee or any sugary drinks, and I have adopted the *vegan* lifestyle. I do not let them give me antipsychotic medication because I am not psychotic.

I am a self-made woman. I earned my own self degrees, bought my own self homes, raised my own self son, and I will survive this temporary setback. I lost my home, credentials, and savings as a result of the court proceedings and the wrongful death lawsuit filed by the woman who initially said, "No English," but that is okay. After all, I have knowledge and my education, and that is something that they can never take away from me. What do you think about that? Hah!

About the Author

IN THIS FICTIONAL NOVEL, THE author reflects upon personal experiences living in a household with a schizophrenic parent. Attempting to fully understand the sequence of behaviors that frightened her as a child, the author delves into the history of the small town in Mississippi that gave birth to her father and the probable experiences that he went through maturing as a black man in the United States Air Force. All these set the stage for the family relationships that ranged from loving to strained. This quest for understanding led to college degrees in behavioral science and counseling and eventually redemption for the anger and pain that molded her decisions and actions from childhood to adulthood.

This is the second publication authored by Geraldine Cynthia Forté. *Appropriating Old Cultures into New Futures* gives the historical and cultural background of the emigration to the state of California from the Kingdom of Tonga in the South Pacific and the impact upon student acculturation and academic success.

The author has served as a K–12 educator in the state of California for over forty years, has taught in the school of education of two universities, and is currently retired. Her passions are writing, piano, growing roses, baking pound cakes, spending quality time with her family, and loving her two Chihuahuas.

CPSIA information can be obtained
at www.ICGtesting.com
Printed in the USA
BVHW081048250219
541082BV00004B/586/P